THE GREAT
DEPRESSION
AND THE NEW DEAL

MILESTONES

IN AMERICAN HISTORY

THE GREAT
DEPRESSION
AND THE NEW DEAL

AMERICA'S ECONOMY IN CRISIS

RONALD A. REIS

CHELSEA HOUSE
An Infobase Learning Company

Chelsea House
An imprint of Infobase Learning
132 West 31st Street
New York, NY 10001

Library of Congress Cataloging-in-Publication Data

Reis, Ronald A.
The Great Depression and the New Deal : America's economy in crisis / by Ronald A. Reis.
   p. cm. — (Milestones in American history)
Includes bibliographical references and index.
ISBN 978-1-60413-766-8 (hardcover)
1. United States—History—1933–1945—Juvenile literature. 2. United States—Economic conditions—1918–1945—Juvenile literature. 3. Depressions—1929—United States—Juvenile literature. 4. New Deal, 1933–1939—Juvenile literature. I. Title. II. Series.

E806.R445 2011
973.91—dc22   2011004462

Chelsea House books are available at special discounts when purchased in bulk quantities for businesses, associations, institutions, or sales promotions. Please call our Special Sales Department in New York at (212) 967-8800 or (800) 322-8755.

You can find Chelsea House on the World Wide Web at http://www.infobaselearning.com

Text design by Erik Lindstrom
Cover design by Alicia Post
Composition by Keith Trego
Cover printed by Yurchak Printing, Landisville, Pa.
Book printed and bound by Yurchak Printing, Landisville, Pa.
Date printed: August 2011
Printed in the United States of America

10 9 8 7 6 5 4 3 2 1

This book is printed on acid-free paper.

All links and Web addresses were checked and verified to be correct at the time of publication. Because of the dynamic nature of the Web, some addresses and links may have changed since publication and may no longer be valid.

CONTENTS

Down and Out

Every morning they would get up, wash up, and dress up. Slacks, a tie, and a jacket made up the wardrobe of the urban worker of the 1930s. For many, it was the only suit they owned, and as a result it was usually threadbare around the collar and sleeves. Still, it was what a man wore, especially one seeking the respect of his fellow workers. Standing at a bus stop, a man could hold his head high as he made his way downtown to earn his livelihood.

That is the impression one strove to convey. Yet in the early 1930s, as the United States fell deeper and deeper into the worst economic collapse in its history, many "workers" were not working. Unwilling to admit the obvious to family, friends, former colleagues, and even themselves, such individuals would pretend to be employed, heading off to "work" in the morning as though nothing in their lives had changed. "The crowd of men waiting for the 8:14 train at the prosperous suburb included many who had lost their jobs and were going to town as usual, not merely to look stubbornly and almost hopelessly for work, but also to keep up a bold front of activity," observed popular social historian Frederick Lewis Allen. "In this latter effort they usually succeeded; one would never have guessed, seeing them chatting with their friends as train-time approached, how close to desperation some of them had come."[1]

The "worker's" day would now be spent hiding in the shadows, aimlessly walking the streets, lounging on park benches, or holed up for hours in a public library, reading the want ads in newspapers. Such a sham, of course, could not last. Soon enough, the begging would start: the borrowing from relatives, many of whom, as time dragged on, became less and less able to lend; the selling off of whatever possessions could be sold; the stretching of credit at the corner grocery store; and the cashing in of a life insurance policy. Finally, if it was available at all, public relief was sought—and with it, the last vestiges of human dignity gone.

Well, almost. When it came to actual survival, to eating, the humiliation could fall still further. "At night people lurked behind restaurants and grocery stores waiting for the refuse cans to be set out, and fought others for the chance to claw through the garbage. They followed sanitation trucks to city dumps. They stared at the food displayed in grocery store and bakery windows and wished they had the nerve to hurl the brick that might let them satisfy their children's hunger for a night."[2]

Throughout it all, in the first devastating years of national economic ruin, President Herbert Hoover would insist no one was actually starving, a statement that was not true. In 1933, the New York City Welfare Council counted 29 deaths from starvation. More than 50 others were treated for acute hunger in hospitals. An additional 110, most of them children, died of malnutrition.[3] "Have you ever seen the uncontrolled trembling of parents who have starved themselves for weeks so that their

The 1929 stock market crash caused a widespread financial crisis called the Great Depression. Millions of Americans lost their jobs and clamored to find any type of available work. Above, men in Newark, New Jersey, stand in line to apply for a job on a construction project in 1935.

children might not go hungry?" asked social worker Lillian Wald.[4] In more than a few cases, fathers were known to hang around street corners while their younger children were fed, lest the "breadwinner" be tempted to eat more than his share.

What soon enough became known as the Great Depression, a calamity to last an agonizing, drawn-out 12 years, was upon the land. Few Americans escaped its consequences.

CRUEL STATISTICS

Herbert Hoover, elected president in 1928, sought, as the nation's economy imploded after the stock market crash of

October 1929, to assign a new name to what was occurring. In an attempt to soothe both public fear and dam the dread spreading on Wall Street, instead of referring to the economic devastation as a "panic" or a "crisis" (as had been done during previous collapses in 1893 and 1907), the president chose to call the current bankruptcy a "depression." Of the three terms, Hoover felt his was the least odious. Regardless of the name, however, government statistics unequivocally exposed a true economic threat—perhaps to the capitalist order itself.

In 1931, 16 percent of the people who wanted work could not find it. By 1933, the number had climbed to 25 percent. In the steel town of Birmingham, Alabama, of 108,000 workers, 25,000 had no jobs, while 75,000 worked reduced hours. Of the latter, the average pay was $1.50 a day (about $25 today). In Detroit, 30 percent of the workers were without jobs. In Chicago it was 40 percent. A whopping 50 percent could not find work across the state of Colorado. New York City was unable to provide employment for 800,000 who desperately wanted it.[5] Only half the nation's engineers had jobs, while 9 out of 10 architects were out of work.

Out-and-out joblessness told only part of the panicky story, however. In unemployment's shadow ran underemployment. "Those Americans lucky enough to keep their jobs saw their hours and pay reduced. . . . By the summer of 1932, more than half of American workers did their jobs part-time, keeping on average 59 percent of a full-time job and of full-time pay."[6]

According to journalist Caroline Bird, much energy was spent simply looking for work. When, in 1931, only 1 out of 50 men applying for an advertised job got it, the other 49 wasted their shoe leather. To such job seekers, a simple hole in the shoe could slow one down to a crawl—or worse. "Maybe it starts with a little hole in the sole; and then the slush of the payment oozes in, gumming socks and balling between your toes," Bird reported a man declaring. "Concrete wets Woolworth socks like a file, and if you turn the heel on top and tear a pasteboard innersole, it won't help much."[7]

By 1933, the nation's gross national product had declined from a 1929 figure of $103,838,000,000 to $55,760,000,000—a plunge of 47 percent.[8]

THE POOR

Because so many Americans were now without work or on severely reduced wages and because so many families, rural and urban, had sunk into desperate poverty, American attitudes toward the poor began to change. Even if one was working, the feeling that at any moment he or she could be next to face the interminable breadlines, the groveling for extended family support, or the meager offerings of infrequent and inadequate government assistance, caused a rise in empathy for one's fellow citizens. With practically everyone experiencing the effects of the shattering economy, being poor took on new meaning.

In the past, there were poor laws and debtors' prisons. The former sought to distinguish between the "deserving" or "worthy" poor, on the one hand, and those on the other who, being of able body and mind, should and could fend for themselves. Debtors' prisons, where a person would be locked up for failure to pay his debts, attempted to act as a deterrent. To the extent that they were successful in encouraging people to pay what they owed, such prisons had a purpose. When they filled up, however, they failed. It became obvious that while in prison, one could not be out working to pay off creditors.

With regard to the poor, the question always remained, was it a societal or a personal failure that they existed at all? Was the system at fault or was one's character to blame? Until the Depression of the 1930s, many felt that the poor were poor because they were lazy, were drunk, or simply lacked ambition. "It was a man's fault if he was poor, that a man ought to take care of his own family and lay aside something for a rainy day."[9] Even in the most dire of economic times, the argument went, an able-bodied man could always work if he was willing to take a lower wage. For him and his family, charity and relief were unnecessary.

Yet now, during the fiercest of economic times, when so many from such varying backgrounds were unable to find work of any kind, a belief in rugged individualism was, of necessity, in need of revision. "The severity of the Depression's misfortune also diminished the distance between the comfortable and the hard-up. So many moved so quickly from one category to another that the employed increasingly identified with their fellow countrymen who were out of work."[10]

To be sure, attitudes were not all that easily changed, even with so many now in the same poverty boat. "The suddenly-idle hands blamed themselves, rather than society. True, there were hunger marches and protestations to city hall and Washington, but millions experienced a private kind of shame when the pink slip came. No matter that others suffered the same fate, the inner voice whispered, 'I'm a failure.'"[11]

With such beliefs still embedded in the American psyche, even with a quarter of the population now without adequate means to buy food or shelter, seeking relief, assuming it was to be had, would be a bitter pill for the unemployed to swallow. No matter how many suffered, being poor in America was still recognized as both a physical and psychological affliction. It was not where people wanted to be.

HUNKERED DOWN

Indeed, being poor could, in the worst case, be out-and-out life threatening.

On Christmas Eve, 1931, the *New York Times* reported that a young couple had left the city, retreated to the Catskill Mountains, entered an abandoned cottage, and, once there, prepared to die. They had gone to the area in search of work, but finding none, and refusing to stoop to begging, preferred, instead, to starve to death. Three days later a policeman discovered the pair, "at which point the wife, age 23, was too weak to walk," the *Times* reported. The paper then went on to declare, "An effort is being made to obtain employment for them, but if this fails they will be sent back to New York."[12]

New York City, a crammed, urban jungle, had, perhaps, more than its share of such desperation, starvation, and suicide. "A father who had been turned away by a New York City welfare agency was afraid to apply for help after public relief had been set up. Social workers found one of his children dead; another, too weak to move, lay in bed with the mother; the rest huddled, shivering and hungry, around the desperate father."[13] In the same city, at about the same time, a dentist and his wife died rather than accept charity. They left a simple note, opened an oven door, and took gas together.

In some parts of the country, notably the South, railroad police would shoot hobos, particularly if they were black, right off the train. As Louis Banks recalled, "We come out of Lima, Ohio . . . Lima Slim, he would kill you if he catch you on any train. Sheep train or any kind of merchandize train. He would shoot you off, he wouldn't ask you to get off."[14]

Of course, not everyone who was down-and-out chose death rather than assistance. Most in poverty took what was offered, were glad to get it, and hunkered down for the long haul as best they could. In the late 1960s, a 45-year-old waitress in Chicago recalled her childhood: "I remember all of a sudden we had to move. My father lost his job and we moved into a double-garage. The landlord didn't charge us rent for seven years. We had a coal stove, and we had to each take turns, the three of us kids, to warm our legs. It was awfully cold when you opened those garage doors. We would sleep with rugs and blankets over the top of us. Dress under sheets."[15]

And, to be sure, there were those who sought, if they could not find steady employment, to earn their daily bread one unconventional way or the other. In 1933, dance marathons took the country by storm. Usually held in armories, most would start with 60 couples. They would dance for 45 minutes every hour, and do so for 24 hours a day. The couples would eat army-style food from boards laid out on sawhorses. The audience came and went. At times, partners took turns sleeping while leaning on each other. "Professional" marathoners, called "Horses," would travel from town to town vying for prize money. "Work" was sought any way it could be had.

BONUS MARCH

As the Depression dragged into its third year, ever more unemployed Americans turned in shame to local relief agencies, most of which had little or nothing to provide. In Toledo, Ohio, each recipient received a daily meal costing less than three cents. In New York City, one averaged a total relief allotment of only $2.39 a week. Even with these meager amounts, it was estimated that only one-fourth of the nation's unemployed were obtaining any relief at all.

Demanding their share, in the spring of 1932 a new category of Americans, war veterans, sought relief as a group. In 1924, Congress had voted to provide World War I veterans with a bonus, the equivalent of a federal pension, to be paid out in 1945, or upon the death of the veteran. For many hungry ex-soldiers, 1945 seemed a long way off. They wanted at least some of the money early. "If the government can pay $2 billion to the bankers and the railroads," one commentator observed, "why cannot it pay the $2 billion to the soldiers?"[16]

Begun with just 300 veterans out of Portland, Oregon, in May, what became known as the Bonus Expeditionary Force (B.E.F.) swelled to 20,000 by the time it stampeded the nation's capital a month later. Disciplined, as would be expected of former army personnel, the veterans, along with wives and children, found "accommodations" as best they could. "There are shelters built of egg crates, of paper boxes, of rusty bed springs, of O.D. blankets, of newspapers, of scraps of junked automobiles, of old wall-paper, of pieces of corrugated iron roofing, of tin and bed ticking, of parts of baby carriages," the *Star*, a local newspaper, reported. "The man who can salvage an auto top from the dump has a mansion in this strange city."[17]

On June 7, 1932, thousands of veterans marched down Pennsylvania Avenue in front of 100,000 cheering onlookers. Even with public opinion sympathetic and in support of the bonuses sought, Congress balked at coming up with the money. President Hoover had made it clear from the start that even if Congress approved payment, he would veto any such legislation.

The situation now turned ugly. Hoover, embarrassed by what the marchers meant to his faltering attempts to revise the economy, ordered the regular army to disperse them. Led by General Douglas McArthur, but aided by Dwight Eisenhower and George Patton (a trio that would go on to distinguish themselves in World War II), the army burned veteran shacks and routed them out with gas. "It was like sons attacking their fathers,"[18] one marcher recalled.

Newsreel footage of the clash between armed and unarmed armies, with tanks rolling through Washington's streets, boded ill for the Hoover administration and for the nation. The images of American soldiers chasing down poverty-stricken veterans merely petitioning their government for relief did not sit well with the country as a whole. With a national election four months away, electoral vengeance promised to be decisive, indeed.

The Roaring Twenties

When World War I (1914–1918) ended, Americans were more than ready to absolve themselves of almost everything continental. "They were fast becoming sick and tired of the whole European mess," wrote Frederic Lewis Allen. "They wanted to be done with it. They didn't want to be told of new sacrifices to be made—they had made plenty."[1] Warren G. Harding articulated the American mode perfectly when he declared early in his presidential campaign, "America's present need is not heroics but healing; not nostrums but normalcy; not revolution but restoration; not surgery but serenity."[2] With his call for "normalcy," President Harding introduced the mantra for the decade and gave voice to Americans who wanted to sit back and relax, and to pursue a new national passion—fun! In what would soon become known as the Roaring Twenties, there would, indeed, be ample pursuit of enjoyment.

In the summer of 1921, on a Washington bathing beach along the Potomac River, a young woman raised eyebrows when, having entered the July Costume and Beauty Show (where contestants wore tunic bathing suits, long stockings, and hats to cover their long, flowing hair), she chose to roll her stockings down below the knees. In September, a similar show in Atlantic City took revelation a step further. "For the time being, the censor ban on bare knees and skin-tight bathing suits was suspended," enthused an astonished reporter, "and thousands of spectators gasped as they applauded the girls."[3] Thus the beauty pageant was born.

Flappers were not far behind. "Such women," noted Lewis, "[w]ore thin dresses, short-sleeved and occasionally (in the evening) sleeveless; some of the wilder young things rolled their stockings below their knees, revealing to the shocked eyes of virtue a fleeting glance of shin-bones and knee-cap; and many of them were visibly using cosmetics."[4]

The 1920s also witnessed the birth of a phenomenon associated with more recent times—the "face-lift." Born out of reconstructive surgery undertaken during the Great War, the more frivolous offshoot soon found a ready customer base. By 1927, no less than 18,000 practitioners had entered the beauty culture business as a whole, launching a new occupation—that of beautician.

It was not all about beauty and relaxed morals, of course. But, clearly, decades before the term took hold, the 1920s had launched a youth culture all its own.

FARMERS' WOES

While life was a party in the cities and industrial centers of America, farmers, who made up nearly one-third of the nation's population, were not having nearly as much fun. In fact, by the decade's end, many were in truly desperate straits.

World War I had been a boon for farmers, especially those who raised wheat. War-torn Europe, its lands lying in ruin, could not raise crops in sufficient quantity to feed both the civilian and military populations. American farmers had eagerly come to the rescue, as they watched government-subsidized wheat prices reach two dollars a bushel. But with the war over, commodity prices plummeted, and along with them farm incomes.

In an attempt to raise revenue, U.S. farmers fell into the trap of overproduction. As they brought additional land into use, more agricultural goods were produced, and prices fell further and further. If an index of farm prices stood at 205 in 1920, it was down to 116 a year later. In the 1920s, hundreds of thousands of farmers left their farms for the cities, seeking the job benefits of rising industrialization.

Adding to their woes, farmers witnessed the effects of a new American diet. In the 1920s, vitamins were all the rage. When families learned that there were vitamins in spinach, carrots, and celery, as well as fruits, they wanted more of these. Some farmers were able to switch to satisfying the new demand, and, along with the invention of better methods of shipping perishable foods, customers thus got what they wanted. Between 1919 and 1928, the acreage of 19 commercial vegetable crops nearly doubled. However, the growers of staples, such as corn, wheat, and cotton, saw demand for their products dive. Furthermore in the new economy of radios, electricity, and automobiles, need for agricultural raw materials fell even further.

Paradoxically, while the market for farm products stagnated or fell, in many parts of the country agricultural land rose in value as Americans flocked to the suburbs. As a result, higher taxes were placed on the increased valuation of the land. Thousands of farmers could not get enough money from their crops to pay the new taxes or to pay interest on the bank loans taken out to keep them above water. With mortgages and loans going into default, banks began to fail. "In seven states of the country, between 40 and 50 percent of the banks which had been in business prior to 1920 had failed before 1929."[5] Bank failures were a bad omen that would come to haunt the early days of the Great Depression.

A WORLD OF DEBT

The 1920s saw, above all, incredible technological innovation and expansion, with the radio and the automobile leading the way. In 1922, total annual sales of "talking furniture," as the radio was often called, amounted to $60,000,000. By 1929, sales had exploded to a staggering $842,548,000—an increase of 1,400 percent.[6] Automobile purchases for the decade nearly doubled, with 4.4 million cars sold in 1929. Motor vehicles were the single most valuable chunk of U.S. manufacturing output.[7] By the end of the decade, there was almost one car for every household in the country.

Clearly, for the nation's growing middle-class population, the American dream seemed close at hand. But could people afford to buy big-ticket items such as automobiles, furniture, household appliances, radios, phonographs, and pianos? In order to purchase an automobile for cash, a typical American family would have to save for almost five years.

Of all the innovations of the 1920s, none was more important in advancing America's standard of living than the advent of widespread installment purchasing. Installment buying allowed one to make a partial payment at the time of sale, with full payment being deferred until some future date.[8] Traditionally shunned as being irresponsible and symbolic of poverty, such stigma soon vanished, with corporate advertising now extolling the virtues of installment purchasing. Companies told perspective purchasers that terms would be "easy to afford," there would be "no strain on your income," it would be "deferred payments you'll never miss," or, "pay the balance like rent, at a rate of a few pennies a day."[9] By the end of the decade, credit was used to procure up to 90 percent of all major durable goods. Americans had found a way to pay for all they deemed as necessities, all that would give them a piece of the pie.

The end of World War I brought great prosperity to the United States, and many technological and cultural advances took place in the 1920s. Radio radically changed communication and entertainment, and women began to defy cultural norms. Above, a woman relaxes and listens to her radio in 1923.

Of course, corporate America not only delighted in the new purchasing patterns, it found them an essential undertaking to keep factories humming. As a result, throughout the decade corporate profits rose 62 percent. Yet with workers' wages in no way keeping up with increased productivity, the question surfaced: Would the middle class be able to keep paying on the installment plan as the bills kept arriving every month?

This enormous output of bargain-priced labor meant that the wealthy who owned and invested in the country's expanding industries only got richer. A Federal Trade Commission

EVERYBODY OUGHT TO BE RICH

In August of 1929, the *Ladies' Home Journal* published an article written by John Jakob Raskob, the wealthy head of the Democratic Party, entitled "Everybody Ought to be Rich." Over the ensuing decades, Raskob, who was also chairman of the General Motors' Finance Committee and the one who established the General Motors Acceptance Corporation (GMAC) in 1919, had taken a lot of heat for what seemed to be an irrational exuberance just three months before the stock market crash that ushered in the Great Depression. However, on closer examination of what Raskob meant by being rich, his views turn out to be more restrained, if not downright conservative.

Raskob begins his article by saying, "[A] man is rich when he has an income from invested capital which is sufficient to support him and his family in a decent and comfortable manner—to give as much support, let us say, as has ever been given by his earnings." For Raskob, being rich meant being able to retire in comfort. If a person, he went on to point out, managed to wisely invest $15 a month starting in 1909, by using a buy-and-hold strategy and reinvesting the dividends paid, he would be worth over $80,000 in 1929. Equivalent to about a million dollars in 2009, this is what Raskob meant by being rich. According to the John Jakob Raskob Web site, "If the title of the article [in the *Ladies' Home Journal*] had been, 'Everybody Ought to Plan for Retirement by Investing in the Stock Market,' perhaps history would have been more kind to him."

Source: "John Jacob Raskob," *The Raskob Web Site,* http://www.raskob.com/jjr.htm

(FTC) study found that the richest 1 percent of Americans possessed an astonishing 60 percent of the nation's wealth.[10] The Brookings Institute noted that .1 of 1 percent of American families (24,000) had an income equal to that of the entire bottom 42 percent (11.5 million).[11]

This unequal distribution of wealth, with so few owning so much, would contribute to exploding speculation by the decade's end—particularly in the stock market.

MARKET MANIA

Although only about 10 percent of the American public actually owned stock in the late 1920s, it seemed to most observers that everyone was buying into corporate America, all with the belief that, according to John J. Raskob, founder of the General Motors Acceptance Corporation (GMAC), "anyone not only can be rich, but ought to be rich."[12] Frederic Lewis Allen keenly observed:

> The rich man's chauffeur drove with his ears laid back to catch the news of an impending move in Bethlehem Steel; he held fifty shares himself on a twenty-point margin. The window-cleaner at the broker's office paused to watch the ticker, for he was thinking of converting his laboriously accumulated savings into a few shares of Simmons. An ex-actress in New York fitted up her Park Avenue apartment as an office and surrounded herself with charts, graphs, and financial reports, playing the market by telephone on an increasing scale and with increasing abandon.[13]

The numbers were, indeed, impressive. Comparing March 3, 1928, stock prices with those of September 3, 1929, American Can went from 77 to $181^7/_8$, AT&T from $179^1/_2$ to $335^5/_8$, General Electric from $128^3/_4$ to $396^3/_4$, and Radio from $94^1/_2$ to an astonishing 505.[14] This stock market activity did not, however, mean that individuals sought to invest in America, to own a piece of a prosperous or promising company. Investors, such as there were, bought stock based on the soundness of the enterprise, expecting the company to do business in the months and years to come in a competent, profitable manner. They were in it for the long haul.

But by 1929, it was speculators, big and little, that were doing most of the stock purchasing. They were out to make a killing by buying stock they expected would go up in price so that it could be sold for a nifty profit. "What you want to get in on is one of the quickly rising stocks of industries that are making the highly demanded consumer goods that are easily available on credit," wrote economist H. Paul Jeffers. "Because the value of your shares is going up every day, the thing to do is to keep your eye on the quotations and unload your stocks at a point that will give you a sweet profit."[15]

If one did not happen to have the cash to purchase these rising stocks, he did what he would have done when buying a car or a washing machine—he bought stock on credit, on the installment plan. With as little as 5 percent down, an enterprising "investor" could pick up almost any stock, planning to pay off the debt when he sold it for a significant profit. Such purchasing, known as "buying on margin," would be a strong contributing factor to the economic disaster about to arrive.

THE STOCK MARKET CRASH

In spite of the stock market's rise in the first half of 1929, the economy was in trouble. In previous years, industry had been overproducing. At the same time, many people were in debt, having borrowed too much money for unproductive purposes. Financier Bernard Baruch wrote: "Whereas it is wise to buy things on the partial payment plan that will result in time in increased economies and better living, at the same time it can be overdone. I am afraid it has now been overdone."[16]

Speculators (and even investors) got increasingly nervous to the point of panic. Reliable stocks were in short supply.

On October 24, 1929, panicked crowds gathered on Wall Street as heavy trading caused the stock market to crash. Known in history as Black Thursday, thousands of people lost everything in a matter of hours.

The Wall Street bubble was expanding and in clear danger of bursting. Those in the know began to wonder: Was it time to get out? "Self-aware fools went into the market assuming that still greater fools had yet to buy in. It took a shrewd judge of national character to decide just when the United States would run through its supply of fools."[17]

The unraveling began in earnest in late October. On October 24, 1929, later to be known as Black Thursday, the market opened steady with prices little changed from the previous day. Then, around eleven o'clock, the deluge broke.

"It came with a speed and ferocity that left men dazed," wrote Elliott V. Bell, an eyewitness. "The bottom simply fell out of the market. From all over the country a torrent of selling orders poured onto the floor of the Stock Exchange and there were no buying orders to meet it."[18]

As bad as Black Thursday was, Black Tuesday, October 29, 1929, was far worse. Even with a bankers' pool pledging $240 million to shore up the market, nothing could now prevent a full-fledged crisis. More than 16 million shares were traded—33 percent more than on October 24. As the ticker tape fell hopelessly behind, trading became completely meaningless. In brokerage houses across the country, individuals discovered that they had not merely lost everything, but were, given their margin purchases, in debt to their broker.

Elliott V. Bell captured the fatalistic mood when he wrote in the *New York Times*:

> Groups of men, with here and there a woman, stood about inverted glass bowls all over the city yesterday [Tuesday] watching spools of ticker tape unwind and as the tenuous paper with its cryptic numerals grew longer at their feet their fortunes shrunk. . . . The crowds about the ticker tape, like friends around the bedside of a stricken friend, reflected in their faces the story the tape was telling. There were no smiles. There were no tears either. Just the camaraderie of fellow sufferers.[19]

The stock market crash of October 29, 1929, did not cause the Great Depression. It was, however, a trigger, a catalyst that would lead to the economic calamity to follow. From that day forward, the 1930s would be synonymous with poverty and despair, a time not only when people would suffer greatly, but when the nation's capitalist system itself would be called into question.

Hooverville

The causes of the stock market collapse in October 1929 have been debated and mulled over for decades. A broad consensus has emerged, however, that recognizes that, after nearly 10 years of spectacular growth, the economy had begun to seriously falter.

The nation's corporate structure rested on shaky ground. Investment trusts used investors' money to speculate in corporate securities. With many such trusts, there was virtually no accountability to stockholders. Some trusts, such as the giant Samuel Unsull Utilities, actually perpetrated fraud and stock manipulation. "As long as profits accrued, these structural deficiencies remained in the background," wrote Roger Biles. "But when the market faltered, many investors found themselves overextended and consequently defaulted on their obligations."[1] Once the market began to implode, and brokers, desperate to cover their loans, demanded payment in full for stocks bought on margin, a crash was inevitable.

The origins of the Great Depression, which followed the stock market collapse, have also been hotly contested over the last three-quarters of a century. While there were numerous factors that worked to plunge the economy into depression, here, there is also general agreement as to cause and effect.

Even with the stock market crashing, 9 out of 10 Americans were not directly affected because they owned no stock. Though it may have seemed at times that everyone was in on the get-rich-quick scheme being perpetrated by Wall Street, it was not so. Farmers, for instance, rarely bought stock, having little money or knowledge to do so.

Nonetheless, the vast majority of Americans did look to the stock market as a bellwether of the nation's economic health. If stocks were rising, to most that meant the economy was growing as well. Conversely, if stocks fell, particularly precipitously, it signaled economic trouble. When Americans witnessed the stock market crash of October 29, 1929, they thought the economy, too, was in a free fall. As economist Joseph Schumpeter wrote: "People felt the ground under their feet was giving way."[2]

Facing a dubious future, Americans now made an important and fateful decision: They stopped buying. "Each signature on an installment-plan contract represented a consumer's prediction about his or her ability to pay in the future. Suddenly Americans no longer felt able to see far enough ahead to make sound forecasts."[3] With purchases declining and with industries reducing output, workers were laid off or had their hours drastically reduced. The economically deprived could no longer buy, pay rent, or invest as before. As the plunge took hold, the economy headed down, down, down.

There were, to be sure, other causes for the Great Depression, including the lack of diversification in industry, an unsettled international economy, the modest state of economic intelligence (knowing what was going on), and bad government monetary policy. But, more than one cause, the key was the self-generating effect of the Great Depression itself. "Each bankruptcy, each suspension of payments, and each reduction of operating schedules affected other concerns, until it seemed almost as if the business world was a set of ten pins ready to knock one another over as they fell; each employee thrown out of work decreased the potential buying power of the country."[4]

LAUGHING IT OFF

What was to follow, the beginning of the greatest economic crisis in American history, occurred on the watch of President Herbert Hoover. Elected just a year before the stock market crash, Hoover and the Republicans expected—indeed, had every right to expect—four more years of President Calvin Coolidge's prosperity. Hoover ran on a platform that promised more of the same.

In the immediate aftermath of the October crash, it was assumed that Hoover had both the skills and the determination to see the country quickly through the downturn and on to renewed prosperity. In the past, Hoover had demonstrated bold leadership in putting into effect polices to help the stricken and less fortunate.

Known as "the Great Engineer," Hoover had served as a relief administrator at the end of World War I, tasked with aiding Europe's recovery. In that position, the future president supervised the distribution of food and clothing to more than 30 million people, which may have saved the lives of 3.5 million children and 5.5 million adults.

As Coolidge's secretary of commerce, Hoover was charged with dealing with the 1927 Ohio flood, the greatest natural disaster the country had yet faced. The deluge, which made refugees of almost a million people, required a huge coordinated response, a challenge Hoover more than met. The publicity surrounding the disaster made him a national hero and propelled him forward to the Republican nomination for president.

When Herbert Hoover (*right*) was elected president, he and his predecessor, Calvin Coolidge (*left*), believed that the prosperity of the 1920s would continue for years. Hoover's lack of response to the stock market crash exacerbated the country's economic crisis.

Yet, his humanitarian inclination and previous actions aside, Hoover was a conservative, and as such believed in the time-honored virtues of "rugged individualism," of neighbors helping neighbors, and of not running to the federal government for help. "This is not an issue as to whether people shall go hungry or cold in the United States," the president declared. "It is a question on the one hand whether the American people will maintain the spirit of charity and mutual self-help through voluntary giving and the responsibility of local government as distinguished, on the other hand, from appropriations out of the Federal Treasury."[5]

Above all, in combating the Depression now upon the nation, Hoover saw himself as a cheerleader to American enterprise, not a coach or, more significantly, a player. Hoover had

HORATIO ALGER JR.

For President Herbert Hoover, the time-honored American values of individualism, hard work, fair play, and the belief that good will, in the end, triumph over evil, were central not only to his personal life, but to the American character. Too much in the way of charity would make citizens soft, the president believed. Hoover may have nurtured such beliefs by reading the novels of the hugely successful nineteenth-century author Horatio Alger Jr. So, too, did millions of Americans who read Alger's uplifting works as they struggled to make sense of the Great Depression that engulfed them.

Alger's principal output was the formulaic juvenile novel that followed the adventures of bootblacks (shoeshine boys), peddlers, newsboys, and buskers (street entertainers)—in other words, the impoverished—in their rise from humble, down-and-out backgrounds to middle-class security and comfort. Their success always came as a result of hard work, clean living, and a dose of good luck.

The author's first novel, *Ragged Dick; or, Street Life in New York with the Bootblacks*, published in 1868, illustrates what would

great faith in the power of words, assurances, and appearances. "No governmental action, no economic doctrine, no economic plan or project can replace the God-imposed responsibility of the individual man and woman to their neighbors," the president intoned in a national radio address a year after the stock market crash. "The Depression," he said, "was a passing incident in our national life and the number who are threatened with privation [poverty] is a minor percentage."[6]

Yet as the nation moved into the second year of what was now clearly a great depression, it became ever more apparent

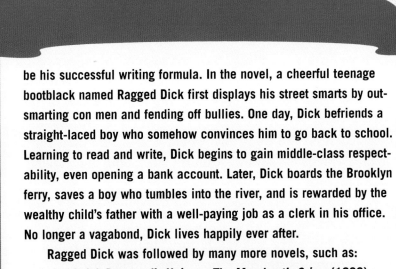

be his successful writing formula. In the novel, a cheerful teenage bootblack named Ragged Dick first displays his street smarts by outsmarting con men and fending off bullies. One day, Dick befriends a straight-laced boy who somehow convinces him to go back to school. Learning to read and write, Dick begins to gain middle-class respectability, even opening a bank account. Later, Dick boards the Brooklyn ferry, saves a boy who tumbles into the river, and is rewarded by the wealthy child's father with a well-paying job as a clerk in his office. No longer a vagabond, Dick lives happily ever after.

Ragged Dick was followed by many more novels, such as:

- *Ralph Raymond's Heir; or, The Merchant's Crime* (1869)
- *Sink or Swim; or, Harry Raymond's Resolve* (1870)
- *Risen from the Ranks; or, Harry Walton's Success* (1874)
- *Sam's Chance; and How He Improved It* (1876)
- *The Store Boy; or, The Fortunes of Ben Barclay* (1887)
- *Striving for Fortune; or, Walter Griffith's Trials and Successes* (1902)

that the crisis of confidence many Americans were facing was not going away, nor could it simply be talked away. When Hoover declared in early 1931, "If someone could get off a good joke every ten days, I think our troubles would be over,"[7] there were not many able to laugh.

RAISING TARIFFS AND TAXES

By the middle of 1932, American industry was operating at half its maximum 1929 volume. At one point, steel production was only 12 percent of capacity. For many farmers, prices had fallen so low that it did not pay for them to harvest their crops; they simply let them rot or burned them for firewood. Deflation had wiped out all the economic gains the country had experienced in two generations. America was now producing no more commodities per capita than it had in the last year of the previous century.[8] The country was in deep trouble.

It is unfair to maintain, however, as some observers have, that Herbert Hoover did nothing to combat the problem but give pep talks and announce that the fundamentals of the economy were sound. Indeed, in 1931 and 1932 the president took action on two fronts that would have a significant effect on the Depression's advance. Unfortunately, both undertakings were a mistake.

On June 17, 1931, Hoover signed the Smoot-Hawley Tariff Act into law. The act raised tariffs (taxes) from 38 to 49 percent, one of the highest rates in U.S. history.[9] In the previous month, 1,028 economists signed an open letter urging the president to veto the legislation. Hoover signed anyway, believing that farmers and industry needed protection from low-cost foreign competition.[10]

Foreign countries, of course, retaliated, raising tariffs on American exports. In the 15 years prior to the act, going back as far as the beginning of the Great War in 1914, America had a favorable balance of payments—sending abroad $25 billion in exports over imports.[11] Such surpluses were now threatened.

The Smoot-Hawley Tariff, as many predicted, soon proved a drag on economic recovery. "A new tariff would shut U.S. sellers off from the world at a time when they badly needed customers," observed Amity Shlaes, a senior fellow in economic history at the Council on Foreign Relations. "It would deprive foreign governments of trade. It would drive the prices of imports up for consumers at home. It would hurt other nations, nations that the United States hoped would become its markets. It would certainly hurt the worker."[12]

Facing an unbalanced federal budget, resulting in part from shrinking tax revenue from business and personal incomes, in 1932, Hoover took another step that would prove unwise: he raised taxes. Believing firmly in a balanced budget, one that would, he hoped, restore confidence with the business community, the president felt he had little choice in signing the Revenue Act of 1932. Individual and corporate levies rose to nearly World War I levels. The tax was placed on manufacturers, who then passed it on to consumers in the form of higher prices—something economically depressed individuals certainly did not need. The U.S. economy fell further and further into depression.

TOO LITTLE TOO LATE

When a person's job went, his home, be it a farmhouse or an urban apartment, was often soon to follow. In Philadelphia, 1,300 evictions took place during a single month in 1931. In New York City, there were 200,000 such ejections for the entire year.[13] When the jobless found their household goods on the sidewalk, on small-town lawns, or in farm lots, they could no longer pretend to be working; their shame was now in full public view for all to see.

While some who were thrown out on the street might find shelter with friends or relatives, many simply had no place to go. In utter desperation, they took up residency in shantytowns, makeshift collections of living space, in vacant lots, at

As the economy got worse and people began to lose their homes, "Hoovervilles" began appearing throughout the country in major cities. These shantytowns were full of people who had lost everything.

railroad junctions, on riverfronts, alongside city dumps, and in parks. People slept in anything they could find or make. Empty piano crates were a luxury. Most of the destitute were content with putting living quarters together with whatever they could scrounge or even steal: cardboard, scraps of metal, and old mattresses being the favorites. Some even lived in city water mains.

Blaming Hoover for their plight, the homeless labeled their new accommodations "Hoovervilles." The president's name soon became identified with additional signs of distress as well.

Jackrabbits and other small game were called "Hoover hogs." Empty pockets pulled inside out were "Hoover flags." "Hoover blankets" were old newspapers used as bedcovers.

The homeless, once shunned as losers and vagrants, were increasingly seen as fellow citizens who had descended into a degradation that might befall almost anyone. Americans readily embraced, with clear understanding, the poignant lyrics of the decade's most popular song, "Brother, Can You Spare a Dime?" Written by E.Y. Harburg, it told of a man who had all his life given to his country and now, down-and-out, wanted a dividend:

> *They used to tell me I was building a dream*
> *And so I followed the mob.*
> *When there was earth to plow or guns to bear*
> *I was always there right on the job . . .*
> *Once I built a railroad, I made it run,*
> *Made it race against time.*
> *Once I build a railroad, now it's done*
> *Brother, can you spare a dime?*[14]

Still, even with the growing evidence of suffering, Hoover's conservative government hung on to the philosophy of minimal interference. The burden of caring for the poor, the administration felt, must rest with local governments or private charity. When the U.S. Chamber of Commerce, a devoutly pro-business organization, polled its members in late 1931, it found that they supported, 2,534 to 197, the proposition that "needed relief should be provided through private contributions and by state and local governments."[15] Hoover agreed.

A NEW DIRECTION

And yet, in 1932, facing a reelection campaign that promised to be an uphill battle, President Hoover reluctantly and timidly reversed himself somewhat and began providing federal help in hopes of rousing the economy. It would not be direct aid to individuals. On that approach the president would not budge—such assistance was to remain a local government and private charity concern and solution. But if support could be provided for business and banking institutions, Hoover was willing to abandon his cherished balanced budget mantra to stimulate the economy from the top down.

In January 1932, the president asked Congress to create the Reconstruction Finance Corporation (RFC), with $500 million in capital and the authority to borrow $2 billion more. The agency would provide loans to banks, insurance companies, and railroads on the theory that what they did with the money would trickle down to the masses, resulting in higher employment. Referred to as "a millionaire's dole" by some, many banks chose to take the money in order to safeguard their assets rather than increase their lending. When the RFC lent $90 million to the huge Central Republic Bank of Chicago while refusing a $70 million loan to the city of Chicago to pay municipal employees and teachers, a public relations disaster struck the president.

In July 1932, Hoover signed a job stimulus bill known as the Emergency Relief and Construction Act. It was to provide $1.5 billion for the construction of public works projects. Like other efforts to spur the economy, however, the Emergency Relief Act proved too little too late.

Hoover's trickle-down economics, where those at the top received stimulus money in the hope that it would filter down to the ordinary citizen below, was severely attacked by the governor of New York, Franklin Delano Roosevelt (FDR). "The present administration," Roosevelt told a huge crowd in April of 1932, "has either forgotten or it does not want to remember the infantry of our economic army. These unhappy times call for . . . plans . . . that build from the bottom up and not from the top down, that put their faith once more in the forgotten man at the bottom of the pyramid."[16]

Roosevelt's "forgotten man" speech went far in ensuring him the Democratic nomination for president at the party's Chicago convention in July. Appearing at the gathering in person, the first presidential nominee of either major party ever to do so, Roosevelt pledged a "new deal" for the American people, one that would undoubtedly involve far more federal government intervention than the current Hoover administration was willing or able to provide.

Franklin D. Roosevelt won the presidency handily in November, collecting 57.4 percent of the popular vote to Hoover's 39.7 percent. The incumbent managed to carry only 5 of the nation's 48 states. Congress went Democrat, too, with a 313 to 117 margin in the House and a 59 to 36 lead in the Senate. No president had ever been so clearly repudiated than Hoover.

In his inaugural address, on a cold, windy, March 4, 1933, President Franklin Delano Roosevelt declared, "So, first of all, let me assert my firm belief that the only thing we have to fear is fear itself—nameless, unreasoning, unjustified terror which paralyzes needed efforts to convert retreat into advance."[17] As Hoover sat passively nearby, the new president went on to declare, "This nation asks for action and action now."[18] No doubt about it, a fundamental change in direction, to a far more activist federal response to the Depression, was about to take place.

A New Deal

Franklin Delano Roosevelt, a distant cousin of former president Theodore Roosevelt, was born into privilege, into the "landed gentry" of Dutchess County, New York. While given the best education aristocracy could provide (attending Groton, Harvard, and Columbia Law School), he failed, nonetheless, to display any academic distinction wherever he enrolled. Yet in 1910, at the age of 28, Roosevelt was elected to the New York State Senate. Soon after, however, he resigned to accept an appointment as assistant secretary of the navy in the administration of the new president, Democrat Woodrow Wilson. Amazingly, in 1920, at the young age of 38, Roosevelt received the Democratic nomination for vice president. Though he ran a vigorous campaign, as did presidential candidate James M. Cox, the ticket lost handily to Republican Warren G. Harding and his running mate, Calvin Coolidge. While Roosevelt failed in his first attempt at national office, his appetite for electoral advancement had been forever whetted. Unforeseen tragedy, however, would delay its fulfillment.

On a sunny day in mid-August 1921, Roosevelt slipped and fell overboard while his yacht cruised off Campobello Island, along the coast of Maine. He suffered a slight chill, but the next day he was back out enjoying his vigorous vacation. Then, according to one account, "In rapid succession Roosevelt went for a swim in a nearby lake, dogtrotted a mile and a half, took a dip in the piercingly cold waters of the Bay of Fundy, and sat in a wet bathing suit for half an hour reading some mail.[1]

The following day, Roosevelt complained of severe pain in his back and legs. He had a high fever. Though a doctor was called, the physician diagnosed only a cold. The next morning, Roosevelt could not walk or move his legs. Another doctor summoned assured the family it was a blood clot or a lesion in the spinal cord. Finally, two weeks later, the true, devastating diagnosis was made; at the age of 39, the future president of the United States had contracted polio, a disease caused by viral infection of the central nervous system. The disease is acute and often crippling, and in its most severe form, it can be fatal.[2]

Roosevelt's bladder became numb; he had to be catheterized. At one time his arms and back were completely paralyzed. Roosevelt suffered from mental depression, while throughout the weeks to come he lay flat on his back, in severe pain.

When he was transferred to the Presbyterian Hospital in New York, doctors became concerned that Roosevelt showed so few signs of improvement. "There was a little motion in the toes of each foot, but the patient could not extend his feet."[3] It is not known exactly when Roosevelt knew for certain that he would never walk again. Throughout the next seven years, he desperately sought a cure. "He spent parts of four winters

Despite contracting polio, Franklin D. Roosevelt was an unstoppable force in politics. Like his distant cousin Theodore Roosevelt, Franklin served as governor of New York and was later elected president of the United States.

on a houseboat off Florida; sometimes he swam and crawled around lonely beaches for hours.[4]

Yet, disabled as he was, Franklin Roosevelt was determined that his infirmity would in no way limit his political aspirations. In 1928, he was elected governor of New York. In 1930, he was reelected. And in 1932, in a landslide, Americans chose Franklin Delano Roosevelt as their thirty-second president. At the time, the vast majority of citizens had no idea that their president was paralyzed from the waist down.

BANKS ON HOLIDAY

Within moments of his inauguration, President Roosevelt was confronted with an array of crises. His response was a group of programs that proposed to produce the "three R's"— relief, recovery, and reform. These programs would be known as the New Deal.

The most pressing of these initial crises was the real danger that, at any moment, the nation's financial system would implode. For the past year, throughout the country, in virtually every state, banks were failing at an accelerated rate. The state of Louisiana closed its banks temporarily out of concern that panicky depositors, fearful of the banks closing their doors, would rush to withdraw their money. In Michigan, the governor ordered all banks closed for eight days. Still, bank failures rippled outward, engulfing state after state. Currency flew out of banks at a rate of $122 million a day. Millions of citizens were losing their life's savings. By inauguration day, 5,500 banks had failed.[5]

On Monday, March 6, two days after assuming the presidency, Roosevelt declared a national banking holiday, closing all banks throughout the country. On Thursday, March 9, he signed the Emergency Banking Act, legalizing the closings. And on Sunday, March 12, Roosevelt went before the American people in the first of what would be 30 fireside radio chats to explain what had happened and why.

"First of all, let me state the simple fact that when you deposit money in a bank, the bank does not put the money into a safe deposit vault," the president declared, "it invests your money in many different forms of credit—bonds, commercial paper, mortgages and many other kinds of loans. . . . A comparatively small part of the money you put in the bank is kept in currency—an amount which in normal times is wholly sufficient to cover the cash needs of the average citizen."[6]

Of course, these were anything but normal times. Banks were failing because they either irresponsibly invested their depositors' money in speculative enterprises, or because, with one-fourth of the workforce unemployed, citizens were defaulting on loans at an unsustainable rate. People, fearful that the banks would not be able to cover savings or checking deposits, rushed to withdraw their money, in cash or in gold. These "runs," as they were called, drained what money a bank had left. The president's banking holiday forced all banks to halt transactions, close their doors, and thus give everyone a breathing spell.

The Emergency Banking Act authorized the Federal Reserve to issue loans to banks, backed by the banks' assets, to flood them with cash to meet depositors' needs. Banks that were financially sound would be allowed to open within a few days. Those less strong would be put under conservators, whose job it was to help restore them to financial health. Banks that could not be saved would be shuttered permanently.

All this government action was designed to restore depositors' confidence and thus get them to return cash to their banks. "I can assure you that it is safer to keep your money in a reopened bank than under the mattress," the president intoned during his 14-minute fireside chat. "We have provided the machinery to restore our financial system; it is up to you to support and make it work."[7]

The next morning, a Monday, people responded positively to the president's plea. Those who had previously lined up to take money out of banks, lined up to put it back in. Within two weeks, 75 percent of the nation's banks were back in business. The immediate crisis was over.

BOTTOMS UP

There was another endeavor for which Roosevelt was prepared to move swiftly, one he saw as a no-brainer. The president was determined to rid the country of one of its most ill-advised experiments—Prohibition.

On January 16, 1920, the Eighteenth Amendment to the Constitution went into effect. It prohibited the manufacture, transportation, and sale of alcoholic beverages throughout the nation. Prohibition was upon the land, and the country was officially "dry." That did not mean, however, that one could not buy a drink. On the contrary, with liquor available in Canada, where it could be purchased at government stores by any adult, bootleggers and rumrunners had a field day smuggling tank loads of liquor over the border. By 1928, the government had spent a whopping $177 million trying to halt the sale of alcohol. Of that sum, coast guard interception alone cost $32 million.[8] All this effort was to little effect, given that a large number of adults were determined to buy and consume alcohol as they wished.

Liquor did not just come across the border, of course— much of it was produced illicitly in the United States. By the mid-twenties, the brewing of booze was taking place in an esti- mated 22 million homes in America. So many were in on the home brewing and distilling process, that someone composed a snappy ditty to summarize each family member's contribution:

> *Mother's in the kitchen*
> *Washing out the jugs;*
> *Sister's in the pantry*
> *Bottling the suds;*
> *Father's in the cellar*
> *Mixing up the hops;*

Johnny's on the front porch
Watching for the cops.[9]

Speakeasies, of which there were an estimated 30,000 in New York City alone, did a bang-up business selling illegal drinks. In such establishments, in order not to draw attention or raise suspicion, a bartender would ask a customer to remain quiet and "speak easy." It was common for police to be bribed by speakeasy operators in order to stay in business.

With Prohibition an obvious failure, Roosevelt was only too happy, on March 23, 1933, to ease the national thirst by

ROOSEVELT'S FIRESIDE CHATS

No one could take command of a radio audience like President Franklin Delano Roosevelt. In the form of what would become know as fireside chats, the president came into the living rooms of millions, beginning on March 12, 1933, and ending on June 12, 1944—30 broadcasts in all. "I never saw him—but I knew him," said Carl Carmer, on April 14, 1945. "Can you have forgotten how, with his voice, he came into our house, the President of these United States, calling us friends . . ."

Below is a listing of the Fireside Chats the president delivered during the 1930s:

1. On the Bank Crisis—March 12, 1933.
2. Outlining the New Deal Program—May 7, 1933.
3. On the Purpose and Foundations of the Recovery Program—July 24, 1933.
4. On the Currency Situation—October 22, 1933.

signing into law a measure that would allow for the sale of beer and wine. On December 5, the Twenty-first Amendment was ratified, in effect repealing the Eighteenth Amendment. In most parts of the country, legalized drinking, both hard and soft, was a public pleasure once more.

AGRICULTURE ADJUSTMENT

When, after his reelection as governor of New York in 1930, Roosevelt began earnestly planning a run for president two years hence, he gathered around him policy experts that could advise him on the issues a presidential candidate should have

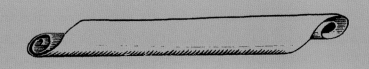

5. Review of the Achievements of the 73rd Congress—June 28, 1934.
6. On Moving Forward—September 30, 1934.
7. On the Works Relief Program—April 28, 1935.
8. On Drought Conditions—September 6, 1936.
9. On the Reorganization of the Judiciary—March 9, 1937.
10. On Legislation to be Recommended to Congress—October 12, 1937.
11. On the Unemployment Census—November 14, 1937.
12. On Economic Conditions—April 14, 1938.
13. On Party Primaries—June 24, 1938.
14. On the European War—September 3, 1939.

Source: Diana Mankowski and Raissa Jose, The Museum of Broadcast Communications, http://www.museum.tv/exhibitionssection.php?page=79

positions on. Most of these counselors came from academia, primarily from universities in the New York area and the East Coast in general. When James M. Kieran, a reporter for the *New York Times*, wrote a brief piece on the group, he dubbed them the "brain trust." The name stuck, and when Roosevelt became president, members of the elite circle were in a key position to suggest major changes as to how the federal government should respond to the deepening Depression.

One such entity established by the brain trust, among a flurry of its creations during Roosevelt's celebrated "first hundred days," was the Agricultural Adjustment Act (AAA). Of all the "alphabet soup" agencies set up between March 9 and mid-June, such as the CCC (Civilian Conservation Corps), the TVA (Tennessee Valley Authority), the FDIC (Federal Deposit Insurance Corporation), and the NRA (National Recovery Administration), the AAA, designed to restore the purchasing power of farmers by eliminating surpluses, would turn out to be one of the more controversial.

The AAA's main purpose was to do something that at first seemed contrary to common sense, if not downright bizarre. The agency would pay farmers not to grow crops or raise animals for slaughter. By either not planting or destroying what had been planted, it was hoped that supply would fall, demand would rise, and farm commodity prices would climb. With nearly half of all Americans making their living directly or indirectly from agriculture, the renewed purchasing power of such individuals, it was argued, would lift up the entire economy. "No nation can long endure half bankrupt," Roosevelt declared, even before his inauguration. "Main Street, Broadway, the mills, the mines will close if half the buyers are broke."[10]

Through the AAA, a program was launched in August 1933 to "remove" from market 6 million young pigs. Though Henry Wallace, the AAA's director, went along with the plan, he was not enthusiastic about it. Be that as it may, Wallace could not understand the national uproar that quickly ensued. "Doubtless

Following his inauguration, Roosevelt worked quickly to provide some relief from the economic crisis. He delivered his first radio "fireside chat" to the American public in March 1933, assuring them that it was safe to keep their savings in banks.

it is just as inhumane to kill a big hog as a little one, but few people would appreciate that," he said. "They contended that every little pig has the right to attain before slaughter the full pigginess of his pigness."[11]

Farmers, too, balked at what they were required to do, even if paid to do so. "It was like slitting your wrist,"[12] one farmer declared. In the South, when horses were first directed to the fields to rip out cotton, accustomed to doing the opposite, they drew back.

In January of 1936, the Supreme Court ruled that the AAA was unconstitutional, based on its supposed abuse of the government taxing authority. Subsidies to farmers, however, remain to this day, with agribusiness now taking in more than $5 billion a year.[13]

THE BLUE EAGLE

On June 16, 1933, the National Recovery Administration (NRA) was created as an industrial counterpart to the AAA. It suspended antitrust laws so that industrial codes, regulating production, prices, and trade practices, could be set up for industry to operate under. As the Depression worsened, businesses were deeply concerned with the "unfair" price-cutting they saw their competitors practicing, in spite of their earnest public support for laissez-faire unfettered capitalism. In some instances, not unlike with farmers, businessmen found that they were manufacturing products that sold for less than the cost to produce them. Under these dire circumstances, brought on by cutthroat competition to attract a receding customer base, industry leaders were more than willing to have the government step in and regulate prices and wages. The NRA stood ready, if not able, to do just that.

To run the NRA, Roosevelt chose General Hugh S. Johnson, a pompous leader of extraordinary dynamism. Known for his salty language and a crude, truculent, strong-willed manner, Old Iron Pants, as he was often referred to, raised conflict wherever he went. He once charged that "only fools and crooks could find flaws in the NRA." The general drank alcohol in awesome binges and would hunker down in his office for days without rest. Johnson kept his name and the name of his agency on the front pages from the moment he assumed command.

Industries that agreed to adopt government codes, or in other ways support the NRA, were allowed to display a poster showing a Blue Eagle, together with the announcement "NRA Member. We Do Our Part." The badge, which was designed by

Johnson himself, represented a thunderbird with outspread wings. Consumers were exhorted to buy products and services only from enterprises displaying the Blue Eagle banner. "When every American housewife understands that the Blue Eagle on everything that she permits into her home is a symbol of its restoration to security," Johnson thundered, "may God have mercy on the man or group of men who attempt to trifle with this bird."[14]

Like the AAA, the NRA was eventually declared unconstitutional by the Supreme Court. In a celebrated case, dubbed "The Chicken Versus the Eagle," by writer Amity Shlaes (but known officially as *Schechter v. United States*), Martin Schechter, a Brooklyn slaughterhouse owner, took on the U.S. Justice Department and won. Schechter, accused of selling unfit chickens, among other NRA code violations, beat the odds with his court victory. The Supreme Court, using the case as a test, determined that the NRA represented an unlawful delegation of power from Congress to the president. With the Court's decision, the Thunderbird all but crashed from the sky—the NRA essentially grounded.

Though Roosevelt publicly expressed his outrage at the Supreme Court's verdict, privately he was to admit that the NRA gave him "an awful headache" and that some of its policies had been "pretty wrong."[15] Though two years after taking office, the president could look back at much that was successful in his New Deal, two of its most ambitious programs, the AAA and NRA, were not part of the triumph.

Frances Perkins

On March 25, 1911, 30-year-old Frances Perkins was taking tea with her friend Margaret Morgan Norrie off Washington Square, in New York City. All around them rose factory lofts, crowded with immigrant workers, many of them young women of Italian or East European Jewish descent. As the two bent to sip their cups of tea, the wails of a fire-engine bell pierced their ears. Within moments, more fire trucks, racing from all directions, descended on an area slightly to the east of where they sat. Abandoning their tea, Perkins and Norrie rushed to the scene, where they soon stood before an unfolding tragedy, one that would not only shock the nation, but alter Perkins's life trajectory.

As Perkins gazed upward, she saw the 12-story Triangle Shirtwaist Manufacturing Company building fully engulfed in flames. Workers, mostly young women, were gathered at the upper windows of the high rise. They were all trying to escape the fire and smoke but were locked in. "People had just begun to jump as we got there," Perkins was to recall later. "They had been holding on until that time, standing in the window sills, being crowded by others behind them, the fire pressing closer and closer, the smoke closer and closer."[1]

Bystanders stood awestruck. "One by one, the people would fall off," Perkins remembered. "They couldn't hold on any longer—the grip gives way."[2] Then came the panic leaping. "People who had their clothes afire would jump," Perkins recalled. "It was a most horrid spectacle. Even when they got the nets up, the nets didn't hold in a jump from that height. . . . They had gone to the windows for air and they jumped. It's that awful choice people talk of—what kind of choice to make?"[3]

In all, 146 workers, the vast majority young Italian and Jewish women, died from this, the worst industrial fire in American history. Perkins was deeply moved, her fury buttressed by the knowledge that but for the installation of simple fire-prevention equipment, the tragedy need not have occurred. Two years earlier, workers of the Triangle Shirtwaist Company had pleaded for help, with the hope of creating a safer working environment. They were not only rebuffed, they were persecuted for complaining.

New York City reacted to the fire with grief, shock, and outrage. A public meeting was called to discuss the event. Perkins was there, sitting attentively in the audience as fiery labor leader Rose Schneiderman, a Russian immigrant, addressed the crowd. "This is not the first time girls have been burned alive in this city," Schneiderman intoned. "Every week I must learn of the untimely death of one of my sister workers. Every year thousands of us are maimed. The life of men and women is so cheap and property is so sacred!"[4]

While many listeners were moved by what Schneiderman had to say, for Perkins the woman's appeal was nothing less than a call to arms. To improve the lot of American workers,

The tragic fire at the Triangle Shirtwaist factory in New York City resulted in the deaths of more than 100 female garment workers. Their deaths sparked a national movement for unionized labor and inspired Frances Perkins, a witness to the tragedy, to push for state labor reforms.

however, she knew a life-long commitment and struggle would be required. Yet Perkins was eager to take up the challenge.

A LIFE'S VOCATION

Born in Boston in 1880, Frances Perkins grew up in an affluent, conservative, and highly religious family. Although a deep faith would comfort her the rest of her life, Perkins soon enough exchanged her parents' conservative values for progressive-era convictions. By the time of the Triangle Shirtwaist fire, Perkins had gathered the tools, through both graduate education and settlement-house exposure, necessary to take up the progressive cause, seeking to better the lives of the downtrodden. "That she was there to see this tragedy [the fire] with her own eyes, to be able to feel it viscerally, is one of history's intriguing strokes of coincidence,"[5] wrote David Von Drehle, author of *Triangle: The Fire that Changed America.*

To pass the kind of legislation necessary to advance factory-working conditions throughout New York, Perkins teamed up with two influential legislators, Bob Wagner and Al Smith, on the newly formed Factory Investigating Commission immediately after the Triangle fire. The commission would hold weekly public hearings and, more importantly, make firsthand, eyewitness visits to plants and mills all over the state.

In one such drop by, commissioners visited an Auburn, New York, rope factory. There they found husbands and wives working alternating 12-hour shifts. The only time husband and wife ever saw each other was when one was on the way in to work, while the other was on the way out. Some would kiss quickly as they passed the gate.

In a Buffalo, New York, candy factory, commissioners saw chocolate boiling over into open gas flames. A single stairway, with no handrail, led to the only exit. There were but two toilets, one of them broken, for 300 workers.

And at a Cattaraugus County cannery, the investigators found children as young as five working alongside their mothers.

When the commissioners asked how long the day was, the answer came back, "Until the children passed out from exhaustion."[6]

The work of the Factory Commission led, in 1913, to the passage of 25 laws that, in effect, recast the labor law of New York, the nation's largest state. "Automatic sprinklers were required in high-rise buildings. Fire drills were mandatory in large shops. Doors had to be unlocked and had to swing outward. . . . To enforce the laws, the Factory Commission pushed through a complete reorganization of the State Department of Labor."[7]

Frances Perkins's work with the Factory Commission propelled her reformist career forward. In 1919, Governor Al Smith appointed her to the New York State Industrial Commission, making her the highest-paid, most influential woman in government anywhere in the United States. Nine years later, when Smith lost his bid to become president, Perkins wisely transferred her loyalty to the newly elected New York governor, Franklin Delano Roosevelt. It would be the beginning of a long, close, and fruitful professional relationship.

SECRETARY OF LABOR

In the four years that Roosevelt was governor of New York, Frances Perkins served his administration in a number of capacities, including that of labor adviser. Still, when the governor was elected president and he looked to fill his cabinet (with a particular concern for who might be his secretary of labor), Perkins's name, at first, drew little support. No woman had ever served in the cabinet of any president. Perkins told her friends and advisers she considered the appointment a long shot.

But Perkins wanted the job, of that there was little doubt. According to Kirstin Downey, author of *The Woman Behind the New Deal: The Life of Frances Perkins, FDR's Secretary of Labor and His Moral Conscience,* "Frances came to realize that the Great Depression could make it possible to take dramatic action on issues she had pondered for two decades. Joblessness and despair had penetrated middle-class society. She realized a consensus for action could be close at hand."[8] Having pushed her reform agenda at the state level, Perkins, now 52-years-old, quickly came to realize that as secretary of labor she could go national with all she wanted to accomplish.

Hundreds of endorsement letters poured into the president-elect's office. Petitions with dozens of signatures arrived. Lincoln Filene, of Filene's Department Store wrote: "I hope that it is true that you are seriously considering her. She is the best equipped MAN for the job that I know of."[9]

Support for Perkins was clearly building. The only serious opposition came from a curious source—top union officials. While they endorsed most of Perkins's goals regarding labor issues and felt her competent to be secretary, they wanted one of their own "men" for the job.

Though Perkins was now clearly on the fast track to becoming secretary of labor (and she knew the appointment would offer her unprecedented opportunity to accomplish her cherished goals), on a personal level, she did have misgivings. The idea of living in Washington supposedly "horrified" her. Paul, her husband, was suffering from mental illness and was in and out of hospitals. Perkins had a strong-willed teenage daughter, Susanna, in her last year of high school. If she accepted the post of secretary of labor, Perkins would be giving up the New York City lifestyle she loved, with its theater and circle of longtime friends from clubs and church. Still, the opportunity to work for her social objectives on the national level was a powerful draw.

On February 22, 1933, Perkins met with the president-elect. "I guess you know what I want you here for," Roosevelt said. "I think you'd be a good Secretary of Labor."[10]

Before accepting, Perkins presented Roosevelt with a to-do list, an itemized account of what she expected him to support as president in the way of progressive labor legislation. It was an ambitious agenda. Perkins wanted to completely reorganize the corrupt Department of Labor. She wanted to do relief and public works. Child labor should be eliminated, she insisted. An eight-hour day and a minimum wage would be at the top of her agenda. Workers' compensation was a must. Unemployment insurance would be necessary. And, above all, some form of an old-age pension plan should be considered.

FEMALE CABINET SECRETARIES

Beginning with Frances Perkins, in 1933, the United States has had 25 female cabinet officers. Most, curiously, have been secretaries of labor, with seven having occupied the position. Three women have served as secretaries of health and human services, with two each in the departments of commerce, education, housing and urban development, and transportation. The departments of defense, treasury, and veteran affairs have yet to see a female secretary.

Presidents Bill Clinton and George W. Bush appointed six women to the cabinet during their respective tenures. In 2009, President Barack Obama named four women to the cabinet—former First Lady and New York senator Hillary Rodham Clinton as secretary of state, former Arizona governor Janet Napolitano as secretary of homeland security, former Kansas governor Kathleen Sebelius as secretary of health and human services, and former California representative Hilda Solis as secretary of labor.

Former North Carolina senator Elizabeth Dole was the first woman to serve in two different cabinet positions in two different presidential administrations. President Ronald Reagan appointed her as secretary of transportation in 1983, and President George H.W. Bush made her secretary of labor in 1989.

Three women have served as secretary of state, the highest-ranking cabinet position. Madeleine Albright was appointed to the position in 1997 by Bill Clinton. Condoleezza Rice became secretary of state in 2005, serving George W. Bush. And Hillary Rodham Clinton took over the position from Dr. Rice in 2009 during Barack Obama's administration.

"Are you sure you want this done," Perkins told Roosevelt, "because you won't want me for Secretary of Labor if you don't want these things done."[11]

Roosevelt told Perkins he would back her, that he had promised the American people change to improve their lives. "He wanted his conscience kept for him by somebody,"[12] Perkins was to recall later.

SOCIAL SECURITY

"Fear," wrote historian T.H. Watkins, was the great leveler of the Great Depression. He said that

> [i]t haunted the dreams of the African-American share-cropper in the South who held a fistful of barren dust in his hand and wondered what the system would do now to cheat him and his family of life. It stalked the middle-class white merchant in Idaho who had seen decades of work destroyed when his once-friendly banker coldly forced him into bankruptcy. It whispered terror into the ear of the Mexican-American foundry worker in Detroit who had put his future in the hands of the coyote who brought him north from Mexico into this strange cold place and who now found his job had vanished. Fear shattered all the fine Anglo-Saxon certitudes of the Great Plains farm wife who watched black clouds of dust roll up on the edge of the horizon and knew that her dreams would soon be sucked up into that boiling mass.[13]

And fear shadowed every worker who looked forward to a retirement where he might have something with which to grow old. Few of the country's 6.5 million people 65 or older had any savings they could draw on after they stopped working. Only 7 percent had any state or private pension plan. Often, seniors turned to charity or relief to survive. Frances Perkins was determined to do something about such conditions.

Having previously worked with Roosevelt at a state level, Frances Perkins was a likely candidate for secretary of labor. Although many believed a man would be a better fit for the job, Perkins's experience and knowledge made her the first woman to serve in a presidential cabinet.

The secretary of labor knew, however, that while in Europe employers and employees contributed to pension systems supplemented by the central government, such a plan, with government contributions, would not fly in America. Perkins looked to the insurance model, one that would insist that any money set aside for old age would be private dollars, contributed by both employees and employers. Roosevelt, Perkins was sure, would want a self-financing plan, one where workers and employers would pay into a fund with a percentage of their paychecks.

On August 14, 1935, after plenty of wrangling and compromising, President Roosevelt signed into law the Social Security Act. At the time, most men died at the age of 60. With Social Security, one could not collect until age 65. Both agricultural and domestic workers were exempt. And yet there was criticism, particularly from the business community. The National Association of Manufacturers called it the "ultimate socialistic control of life and industry."[14]

While Roosevelt gets almost all the credit for Social Security, it was his secretary of labor who backed and then pressed the program forward, often against tremendous odds. "The one person, in my opinion, above all others who was responsible for there being a Social Security program in the early thirties was Frances Perkins," said Maurine Mulliner, an assistant to then-senator Robert Wagner. "I don't think that President Roosevelt had the remotest interest in a Social Security bill or program. He was simply pacifying Frances."[15]

WEST COAST SEAMEN'S STRIKE

Secretary of Labor Frances Perkins was, of course, primarily concerned with labor issues—the demands of laboring people for union representation and better working conditions. After a steady decline in labor influence in the openly pro-business Republican administrations of the 1920s, under Roosevelt and a Democratic Congress labor took heart and began fighting for worker influence. As a result, throughout the thirties, labor agitation, strikes, and, in many cases, violence, spread across the land. Secretary of Labor Perkins was actively involved in many of the resulting labor disputes, often acting as the calming voice, one promoting arbitration and compromise. In this regard, Perkins was no more effective than when she mediated the largest employee walkout of the decade—the 1934 West Coast Waterfront Strike.

In early 1934, West Coast maritime workers (longshoremen and seamen) began actively agitating for a redress of long-held grievances. They wanted more money. They wanted shorter hours. And, above all, they wanted elimination of what they considered a slave-market process whereby they were hired each day by a foreman who doled out jobs to men in return for kickbacks. Instead, dockworkers wanted the establishment of hiring halls where they could wait indoors to be matched with jobs.

Failing to get any of their demands met, on May 9, 1934, longshoremen in every West Coast port walked out. Sailors joined them a few days later. On Thursday, July 5, police called in to break up the strike on the Embarcadero, in San Francisco, fired on a seaman and a strike sympathizer, Nicholas Bordois and Howard Sperry, killing them both. The following day, thousands of strikers, families, and sympathizers took part in a huge funeral march, tramping nine abreast down Market Street. On July 14, a general strike was called, the first in the nation's history. Business activity throughout the city ground to a halt. One hundred and thirty thousand workers stayed home.

The mayor of San Francisco declared a state of emergency. The governor activated the National Guard. While Roosevelt was out of reach (on tour of the Pacific Fleet), Secretary of State Cordell Hull, who was standing in for the president, called Secretary of Labor Perkins, informing her that he was thinking seriously of calling out the army.

Perkins stalled for time, insisting that arbitration be given a full chance. The situation cooled. In a day or two, as the secretary of labor had predicted, workers by the thousands went back to work. In response, employers gave ground and agreed to arbitration. "Ultimately the longshoremen won their hiring hall, better wages, and improved working conditions," reported Kirstin Downey. "Face had been saved all around."[16] In the process, too, Frances Perkins made it clear that she was fully in charge, and that the "Madam Secretary" would be a force to reckon with in the labor ferment to come.

Employment Programs

When Franklin Delano Roosevelt took office in the spring of 1933, 38 percent of nonagricultural workers were unemployed. In Toledo, Ohio, four of every five breadwinners were without jobs. While the New Deal, in the period 1933 to 1935, did moderate suffering in the lives of many families, the Depression remained a dark force throughout the land.

With no end of economic adversity in sight, belief in what it took to succeed in America was being called into question, again and again. "The American Dream," based on the premise of limitless opportunity and economic abundance, seemed less and less something to hold on to. "The Depression weakened many Americans' most common assumptions: that reverses in the business cycle were brief and temporary, that jobs would always be available to those willing to work, that businessmen were the oracles and seers of society, that the younger generation would always be able to come up in the world and do better than its parents," wrote cultural historian Morris Dickstein. "There had been many earlier recessions and even depressions in the American economy, but none had lasted so long and cut so deep."[1]

It was not long before Americans everywhere were turning to barter as a means of economic exchange and survival. Some such entities for swapping goods and services even issued their own scrip (money). In Seattle, Washington, "The unemployed cut unsalable timber for fuel, dug up unsalable potatoes, apples, and pears, ran idle fishing boats, and distributed unsold fish in exchange for the services of doctors, barbers, carpenters, cobblers, and seamstresses," reported Caroline Bird. "At Christmas, an unemployed Santa Claus distributed toys made by the unemployed workers to the children of unemployed fathers."[2]

In Berea, North Carolina, a farm woman recalled, "We didn't have money for postage stamps, so we put the letter along with two eggs in the mailbox and paid the postman that way."[3]

As joblessness continued its relentless drone, and as more and more men were thrown out of work and forced to grovel for food in breadlines, there were those who looked around and thought they saw a way out, or at least a way to mitigate the unemployment toll on the mainstay of family support—the father. "Employed wives," a civic group in Chicago declared, "are holding jobs that rightfully belong to the God-intended providers of the household." Women, the argument went, were primarily working for pocket money. A congresswoman named Florence Kaha went so far as to say, "Woman's place is not out in the business world competing with men who have families to support." A poll showed that 82 percent of Americans agreed. Forty percent said that women should not hold jobs even if they were the sole support of the family.[4]

Banks and factories began to dismiss married women. In three of four cities, wives were excluded from teaching positions. Congress passed a law that forbade two married persons

to work for the federal government. Eighty percent of those fired were wives.[5]

With opinions like these, no wonder Americans eagerly embraced what would clearly become the most popular jobs program the Roosevelt administration ever created. Even those who would vehemently oppose virtually everything the president tried to do in attempting to reduce unemployment would find little to criticize in the establishment and running of the Civilian Conservation Corps (CCC), a virtually all-male natural resource protection and jobs program that in its nine years of operation put (albeit for relatively short durations) 3 million young men to work.

THE 3C'S BOYS

On March 21, 1933, the president sent a proposal for the Civilian Conservation Corps to Congress. A mere ten days later, the program that would put to work unemployed men between the ages of 18 and 25 to plant trees, drain swamps, construct reservoirs, build dams, and generally refurbish forests, parks, and beaches was up and running. Roosevelt claimed that the CCC would not only conserve and replenish the nation's natural resources, it would build sturdy bodies and elevate the sprit of youth from the blighted cities where most participants would come from.

The CCC would be run with the assistance of the Department of Labor (to do the recruiting), the Interior and Agriculture departments (to supervise projects), and the War Department (to run the military-style camps). In order to join, one had to be unmarried, come from a family on relief, and commit, in most cases, to a two-year stint. Each enrollee was to be paid $30 a month, of which $25 had to be sent home to their families. All food, clothing, and other necessities would be provided.

For many of the young men who served in the 3Cs, the experience would be life changing. Hard times and the lure

Roosevelt established the Civilian Conservation Corps (CCC) in an effort to alleviate unemployment for young men. Those who worked with this organization provided manual labor to help rebuild and conserve the country's natural resources. Above, members of the CCC build a fence.

of adventure drew most of them. And while enrollees would initially complain about the food and living conditions, most soon learned to adapt and even thrive. "Many corpsmen from the cities had never been out of earshot of the rumble of trucks and trains or the clatter of horsecarts," wrote Nick Taylor.

> They had never slept out of doors, swum in running streams, or seen beyond the city lights to the stars of the Milky Way splashed across the night sky. They discovered a different

country and a different world as they built fire observation towers, cleared firebreaks, planted trees by the millions to halt erosion, thinned overgrown forests, stocked fish, cleaned up and improved historic battlefields, and built shelters, paths, and camping areas. Most of them put on weight and added muscle.[6]

By April 10, barely a month after Roosevelt had been inaugurated, the original CCC quota of 25,000 youth had been met. By July 1, 1,300 CCC camps were under construction and filled with 274,375 enlistees. Supervisors, camp officers, foremen, and doctors were drawn from the military and civilian populations to run the CCC camps. Such individuals became role models for the young volunteers.

Fun, work, and adventure seemed the main draw for city youth. "Before enlisting, all of us had been burdened with the same Great Depression hopelessness of a life without jobs and income," wrote Edwin G. Hill, an early CCC participant. "Obviously, we were thankful for the $5 spending money we received each month, and for the $25 monthly allotment sent home to help our families through those lean years."[7]

By the time the CCC program ended, the vast majority of its 3 million participants would come to feel the same.

"WE CAN TAKE IT"

Frank C. Davis remembers his first day as a CCC volunteer, assigned to Company 411, Camp NP5, in the Great Smoky Mountains National Park, North Carolina. "Our job was to build fire trails throughout the mountains to give access for firefighters to combat forest fires, and to build hiking trails for recreational use," he begins in his delightful remembrance, *My C.C.C Days: Memories of the Civilian Conservation Corps.*

> At 8:00 a.m. we left the camp and started walking to the job. As the trail progressed, the work area became farther

and farther from the camp. On this day we walked for three hours before reaching the work site. We worked for one hour and then stopped for lunch. Our lunches were brown bags picked up that morning when leaving the mess hall. They were all alike, of course, consisting of a baloney sandwich, a cheese sandwich, a peanut butter sandwich, and a jelly sandwich. Peanut butter and jelly were my favorite, so I traded my baloney sandwich and my cheese sandwich for another peanut butter and another jelly. Putting them together I had two extra thick peanut butter and jelly sandwiches.[8]

ELEANOR ROOSEVELT

Eleanor Roosevelt was one of the most influential women of the twentieth century, and certainly the most noteworthy (and controversial) First Lady. During her husband's long presidency, Eleanor traveled extensively around the nation, in particular surveying working and living conditions, visiting relief projects, and then reporting her observations back to the president. After President Roosevelt's death, in 1945, Eleanor continued her public service, most notably as a U.S. delegate to the United Nations from 1945 to 1953, and again in 1961.

Throughout her adult life, Eleanor Roosevelt wrote extensively. Below are some of her more notable quotes:

- *A little simplification would be the first step toward rational living, I think.*
- *Anyone who knows history, particularly the history of Europe, will, I think, recognize that the domination of education or of government by any one particular religious*

Davis goes on to recall a day drilling holes by hand for dynamite charges. "The dynamite crew was a three-man crew consisting of one man who held the long steel drill while the other two took turns driving the drill with sledgehammers. The man holding the drill was called the steel shaker. He had to turn the drill a quarter turn each time it was hit. He was the bravest, for heaven help him if one of the other two missed."[9]

It was not all work for the 3C's boys, of course. Davis remembers a time when a U.S. Army chaplain came to his camp to put on a demonstration of hypnotism.

> faith is never a happy arrangement for the people.
> - *Campaign behavior for wives: Always be on time. Do as little talking as humanly possible. Lean back in the parade car so everybody can see the President.*
> - *Do what you feel in your heart to be right—for you'll be criticized anyway. You'll be damned if you do, and damned if you don't.*
> - *Friendship with one's self is all important, because without it one cannot be friends with anyone else in the world.*
> - *Happiness is not a goal; it is a by-product.*
> - *Hate and force cannot be in just a part of the world without having an effect on the rest of it.*
> - *Great minds discuss ideas; average minds discuss events; small minds discuss people.*

Source: Brainy Quote, http://www.brainyquote.com/quotes/authors/e/eleanor_roosevelt_2.html

He brought one of the boys under his spell and told him it was freezing cold in there. The boy started shivering and we kept handing him coats to put on. Then he was told that it was very warm in the place and he started sweating and shedding the coats. Next he was told he had a severe toothache. That was a mistake. Aside from groaning he came out with some very bad profanity. The chaplain quickly brought him out of it and never hypnotized us again.[10]

The list of CCC accomplishments runs long and deep. From its inception in 1933 to its dismantling on the eve of World War II, the list includes:

38,087 vehicular bridges
26,368,296 rods of fencing
83,548 miles [134,457 km] of new telephone lines
23,725 new water sources
122,169 miles [196,612 km] of truck trails and minor roads
5,875,578 erosion check dams
2,246,100,600 trees planted
3,998,328 acres [1,618,066 hectares] of forest stand
    improvement
6,304,211 man days fighting fires
6,192,269 man days of fire presuppression and prevention
20,934,581 acres [8,471,924 ha] of trees, plant disease, and
    pest control operations.[11]

The Civilian Conservation Corps, whose motto was, "We Can Take It," has a legacy appreciated to this day. Indeed, in the twenty-first century, numerous state-sponsored CCC offshoots and recreations exist throughout the country.

WORKS PROGRESS ADMINISTRATION

On April 8, 1935, Congress passed the Emergency Relief Appropriations Act, giving the president $4.8 billion to set up almost any conceivable project that would further the public good. Roosevelt used the bulk of the money to establish the Works Progress Administration (WPA), the biggest and best-known work relief program of the New Deal. The president called the WPA the most comprehensive work plan in the history of the nation and assured Americans that all manner of work would be undertaken.

The program drew immediate criticism for spending money on what some felt were useless projects. The agency, headed by Harry Hopkins, would wind up, over its eight-year period, dispensing nearly $11 billion and hiring 8,500,000 persons to build schools, playgrounds, hospitals, and even airports. It would employ artists, writers, and actors.[12] Roosevelt wanted the WPA to enlist as many people as possible, as quickly as possible, to reduce unemployment. To do that, the WPA could not do what private enterprise was doing or what local governments did, otherwise it would be taking jobs out of those sectors, jobs that already existed. Thus it was understandable that some WPA projects would seem like the kind that would not ordinarily get done. Some called such undertakings useless, make-work projects.

"Usefulness," however, was in the eye of the beholder. "Black children in the Beaver Dam section of Bleckley County, Georgia, might have understood usefulness in terms of paint on the walls of their tumbledown school, resting the building on columns of bricks rather than stacked fieldstones, a coal stove that actually provided heat, and glass windows to keep it in and the bugs out instead of the warped shutters of raw board that were there now," wrote Nick Taylor, author of *American-Made*. "The citizens of New Straitsville, Ohio, would have thought useful meant putting out the fire that had been burning in the coal shafts under their homes for more than fifty years. . . . Social workers in Milwaukee and many other cities dreamed of brightening the lives of poor children by refurbishing discarded toys. Therapists at hospitals believed murals on walls would help patients to recover."[13]

The Works Progress Administration was the largest agency formed under Roosevelt's New Deal. This public works organization employed thousands of people in a variety of projects, including painting murals, improving public buildings, and constructing playgrounds and roads. Above, artist Allen Saalburg directs WPA muralists.

Often, a WPA project that looked extravagant at first glance, such as a $25,000 dog pound for Memphis, Tennessee, turned out to serve a useful purpose. The pound in question, it was determined, reduced the number of dog bites and treatments for rabies.[14]

Harry Hopkins had little patience with those who were critical of what the WPA sought to accomplish, of individuals who wanted to postpone WPA work relief to see if other programs would "work out" first. "People don't eat in the long run," he shouted in a memorable quote, "they eat every day."[15]

EATING EVERY DAY

In response to a board of aldermen hearing in New York City to investigate the spending of New Deal relief funds, the *New York Times* reported: "$3,187,000 Relief is Spent Teaching Jobless to Play." Right below the headline, a subhead declared, "Boon Doggle's Made."[16] Thus entered into the vocabulary of the nation a word (boondoggle) that would come to define, in critics' eyes, all that was wrong with the "socialist," "make-work" projects of the Roosevelt administration.

In the aldermen hearings, Robert Marshal, a training specialist and craft teacher from Brooklyn, was called to testify. Marshal told the committee that he taught "boon doggles." When asked to clarify, the teacher replied, "I spend a good deal of time explaining it. Boon doggles is simply a term applied back in the pioneer days to what we call gadgets today—to things men and boys do that are useful in their everyday operations or recreations or about their homes."[17] The committee immediately seized on the word *boondoggle* to signify what they thought was useless, something done by the government that is pointless and wasteful of money.

Criticism centered on the image of "shovel leaners" and "leaf rakers," workers that supposedly just loafed around in their make-work world of "work." In response, a WPA laborer wrote a poem:

> We've made a lot of lovely things.
> Just leaning on a shovel;
> Parks with flowers and sparkling springs,
> Just leaning on a shovel.
> The winding roads and the highways straight,
> The wonderful buildings that house the great,

We built them all at our lazy gait,
Just leaning on a shovel.[18]

Nowhere was there more criticism than when the WPA expanded its work programs to include artists, writers, performers, and white-collar workers in general. The Federal Theater Project (FTP) is a case in point. Headed by Hannie Flanagan, an old friend of Harry Hopkins, the FTP would come to employ 12,700 theater workers in 31 states and New York City. In its four-year history it produced 1,200 plays, a number of them criticized for their supposed socialist, even communist leanings. The FTP would put on more than 1,000 performances a week for an estimated audience of nearly a million.[19]

When Hopkins told Flanagan that it would not be easy to spend the peoples' money, he made it clear that no matter what she did she would always be wrong. "If you try to hold down wages, you'll be accused of union-busting and grinding down the poor ... if you scrimp on production costs, they'll say your shows are lousy; and if you spend enough to get a good show on, they'll say you're wasting the taxpayers' money. Don't forget that whatever happens, you'll be wrong."[20]

In the end, still addressing Flanagan, Hopkins summed up the WPA's purpose, "What's a government for, if not providing jobs when the private sector failed? Why we've got enough work to do right here in America ... to lay out a program for twenty years and to employ every unemployed person in the country to carry it out."[21] Putting people to work, providing jobs, jobs, jobs; this is what the Roosevelt administration and the New Deal were all about.

The Dust Bowl

For farmers, a group consisting of more than a fifth of the country's working population, the Great Depression began a decade earlier than for others—soon after World War I ended. Overproduction and falling demand resulted in a drastic drop in farm commodity prices. For most, production costs exceeded income. As farmers (particularly in the Midwest) saw their situation growing more desperate with every passing season, many felt it was time to take direct, "political" action.

On May 3, 1932, while Hoover still sat in the White House, despondent farmers in Des Moines, Iowa, gathered to say enough was enough. Lead by fiery activist Milo Reno, they declared their intent to hold back product in the hope of increasing demand, and thus prices. The farmers declared a "holiday" from farming. The newly formed Farmer's Holiday

Association (FHA), operating under the slogan "Stay at Home—Buy Nothing—Sell Nothing," vowed to withhold pork, beef, corn, and milk until the federal government addressed their grievances. Though government action was what members demanded, the organization's unofficial theme song made it clear that their real target was the nation's bankers:

> *Let's call a farmer's holiday*
> *A holiday let's hold;*
> *We'll eat our wheat and ham and eggs*
> *And let them eat their gold.*[1]

In the struggle to keep fellow farmers in line with their holiday objectives, association members took to prowling rural roads in an attempt to intercept a "stubborn" farmer's goods on the way to market.

"On a paved road in northwestern Iowa, a truck loaded with cream cans bowls along," began Donald R. Murphy in an article in the *New Republic* of August 31, 1932. "Suddenly a long-chain stretched between two trees bars the road. From the sides of the highway, where they have been lounging under the trees in the tall grass, a dozen tanned men, the leader waving a red flag, bar the road. There are pitchforks handy for puncturing tires, rocks for cracking windshields, and clubs to persuade the truck driver."[2] Within minutes the farmer's buckets had been dumped all over the road.

The Farmer's Holiday strike plan was doomed to ultimate failure, however. When prices rose slightly, farmers, being independent souls, rushed to sell their products once more, and down went prices again.

Farmers had better luck stopping the bankers in attempts to foreclose on farms and repossess livestock. With the sheriff standing at his side, a banker would hold a sale of land and goods to a crowd's highest bidder. Farmers soon got wise to what was going on. Pretty soon they would show up en masse to form a "penny auction," where they would bid a dime for a horse, a cow, a combine, and so on. Any farmer who attempted to bid higher would be "dealt with" later on. The purchased goods were later returned to the threatened farmer. These 10-cent sales worked for a while, keeping more than a few last-ditch farmers working their land.

In one incident of note, in Le Mars, Iowa, a judge declined to side with farmers, refusing to swear he would not sign any more foreclosures. A crowd of more than 600 farmers attacked the judge, blindfolded him, and carried him in a truck a mile (1.6 km) from the city, where they put a rope around his neck. Though they did not hang the judge, his face was smeared with grease and his trousers were stolen. It was a tense, intimidating time.

DARK CLOUDS RISING

It was not only economic conditions that conspired to depress the American farmer in the fourth decade of the twentieth century. Nature contributed a devastating blow as well.

"We could see this low cloud bank it looked like," said J.R. Davison, in the film *Surviving the Dust Bowl.* "You could see it all the way across. And we watched that thing get closer. Seemed to kind of grow you know and it was getting closer. The ends of it would seem to sweep around. And you felt like you know you were surrounded. Finally, it would just close in on you. Shut off the light. You couldn't see a thing."

"And it kept getting worse and worse," added Melt White, as part of the film's narration:

> And the wind kept blowing harder and harder. It kept get-ting darker and darker. And the old house is just a-vibratin' like it was gonna blow away. And I started trying to see my hand. And I kept bringing my hand up closer and closer and closer and closer. And I finally touched the end of my nose and I still couldn't see my hand. That's how black it was. A

In addition to the Great Depression, the Midwest began experiencing devastating dust storms that lasted for seven years. A direct result of poor agricultural practices and a drought, this period would be known as the Dust Bowl.

lot of people got out of bed, got their children out of bed. Got down praying, thought that was it. They thought that was the end of the world.[3]

It was the beginning of what would be called the "Dirty Thirties," a seven-year period when the nation's Great Plains would experience the worst drought in its history. The area, soon to be called the Dust Bowl, would see storms that could draw up dirt clouds 15,000 feet (4,572 meters) high. In one particularly devastating storm, soil rose so high that airplane pilots reported having trouble climbing fast enough to escape the onslaught. The storm was 900 miles (1,448 km) wide, 1,800 miles (2,896 km) long, and gathered up an estimated 300 million tons (272 million metric tons) of farmland—3 tons (2.7 metric tons) for every man, woman, and child alive in the United States at the time.

Given such destruction, economic and natural, it's no wonder that many Midwest farmers found it impossible to go on. They saw their seeds being drawn out of the ground, trucks being blown 30 to 40 feet (9 to 12 meters) down a street, and chickens going to roost in the middle of the day because a dust storm made it so dark the chickens thought it was night.

In the end, hundreds of thousands of farmers saw no choice but to leave. Given the severity of the Great Depression all around, they at first puzzled over where to go. Eventually, the answer would become clear enough—go west, as their forefathers had done—to the land of sunshine and abundance. Midwest "exodusters" would head for California.

CALIFORNIA DREAMING

It would not be easy, leaving a land one may have homesteaded— a land one had worked a lifetime to bring into fruitful production. Packing up everything, as little as that may have been, and heading west on a mere promise would be life wrenching. Yet for no less than one million farmers and their families from Oklahoma, Texas, Arkansas, and Missouri, there was no alternative but to try someplace new.

California, forever seen as a promised land, would be the most popular destination for Great Plains migrants. Handbills that advertised the need for farmworkers in the "golden fields" of California's agricultural "paradise" lured folks west. "300 WORKERS NEEDED FOR PEACHES—PLENTY OF WORK— HIGH WAGES AND 500 MEN FOR COTTON—NEEDED NOW!—START WORK RIGHT AWAY!"[4] they declared. In enthusiastic response, "Okies" and "Arkies" cried out, "Goin' to Californ-I-A! Goin' to Californ-I-A!"

Route 66, the highway that ran 2,400 miles (3,862 km) from Chicago to Los Angeles, would be the avenue to carry the majority of those fleeing parched lands. "The Mother Road—the Road to Flight," author John Steinbeck called it.

"The dispossessed were drawn west from Kansas, Oklahoma, Texas, New Mexico; from Nevada and Arkansas, families, tribes,

WOODY GUTHRIE

Woody Guthrie, born in Okemah, Oklahoma, on July 14, 1912, was, by all accounts, the real thing—a man of the people, an Okie among Okies. He wrote more than a thousand songs, though many sold few copies. His most famous ballad, "This Land Is Your Land," a classic protest song, became, in effect, the country's alternate national anthem. In it Guthrie cries:

> In the squares of the city, In the shadow of a steeple;
> By the relief office, I'd seen my people.
> As they stood there hungry, I stood their asking,
> Is this land made for you and me?

In his autobiography, *Bound for Glory*, Guthrie told of his bond with the downtrodden:

> I was thirteen when I went to live with a family of thirteen in a two room house. I was going on fifteen when I got me a job shining shoes, washing spittoons, meeting the night trains in a hotel uptown. I was a little past sixteen when I first hit the highway and took a trip down around the Gulf of Mexico, hoeing figs, watering strawberries, picking mustang grapes, helping

dusted out, tractored out," Steinbeck declares in his master-piece, *The Grapes of Wrath.*

Carloads, caravans, homeless and hungry; twenty thousand and fifty thousand and a hundred thousand and two hundred thousand. They streamed over the mountains, hungry

carpenters and well drillers, cleaning yards, chopping weeds, and moving garbage cans.

Soon after Guthrie experienced "Black Sunday," the nation's worst dust storm, firsthand, he sat down to pen his most memorable line, "*So long it's ben good to know yuh.*"

Upon arrival in California, in the summer of 1938, Guthrie took to wandering about singing to migrant workers. As he hitchhiked from camp to camp, he came up with what would be one of his most notable songs, "Dust Bowl Refugees." The first verses summed up the migrants' plight:

Cross the mountains to the sea,
Come the wife and kids and me.
It's a hot old dusty highway,
For a dust bowl refugee.

No doubt about it—Woody Guthrie was the real thing. He died in 1967, after a long bout with a hereditary brain disease.

Source: Ronald A. Reis. *The Dust Bowl.* Chelsea House Publishers, 2008.

and restless—restless as ants, scurrying to find work to do—
to lift, to push, to pull, to pick, to cut—anything any burden
to bear, for food. The kids are hungry. We got no place to
live. Like ants scurrying for work, for food, and most of all
for land.[5]

Roads such as Route 66 were not the only way to California,
of course. There were also the railroads, particularly the
Southern and the Santa Fe. If a farmer was without money,
single, or actually willing to abandon the family, he could hop
a train, but he would have to sneak aboard and ride with the
freight. He would become a hobo, a rider of the rails.

At first, many hobos, particularly youngsters, thought they
were off on a great adventure. "One day when school got out—
it was the month of June, in 1934, me and another guy caught
the first train out," said Guitar Whitey. "There was about
twenty guys in the box car and they had to help us up 'cause I
couldn't even reach the floor."[6]

Soon enough, however, the life of a hobo often turned to
loneliness and despair. Jimmie Rodgers, later to be dubbed
"The Father of Country Music," summed up the rail rider's
dejection in his song *Waiting for a Train*:

> *Nobody seems to want me, or lend me a helping hand,*
> *I'm on my way from Frisco, I'm going back to Dixie land;*
> *Though my pocketbook is empty, and my heart is full with pain,*
> *I'm a thousand miles away from home, just waiting for a train.*[7]

THE GRAPES OF WRATH

John Steinbeck, more than any American writer, poignantly
chronicled the plight of migrant workers as they entered California, only to discover a land of limited, not limitless, opportunity. "They arrive in California usually having used up every
resource to get here, even to the selling of the poor blankets
and utensils and tools on the way to buy gasoline," he wrote in

the *San Francisco News* of October 1936. "They arrived bewildered and beaten and usually in a state of semi-starvation, with only one necessity to face immediately, and that is to find work at any wage in order that the family may eat."[8]

In his most famous novel, *The Grapes of Wrath*, published in 1939 (made into a hugely successful movie the following year), Steinbeck depicts in compelling prose just what awaited Dust Bowl migrants and others hoping to flee the poverty of Midwest Depression America. Referring to an agricultural contractor, a worker declares:

> Maybe he needs two hundred men, so he talks to five hundred, an' they tell other folks, an' when you get to the place, they's a thousan' men. This here fella says, 'I'm payin' twenty cents an hour.' An' maybe half a the men walk off. But they's still five hundred that's so goddamn hungry they'll work for nothin' but biscuits. Well, this here fella's got a contract to pick them peaches or—chop that cotton. You see now? The more fella's he can get, less he's gonna pay. An he'll get a fella with kids if he can."[9]

Steinbeck becomes his most forceful and revealing when he describes migrant camps and those that live in them. "From a distance it [the camp] looks like a city dump, and well it may be, for the city dumps are the source of the materials of which it is built,"[10] the author declares in his "The Harvest Gypsies," for the *San Francisco News*. Steinbeck then goes on to divide camp residents into three groups. The first, at the top of the hierarchy, is a farm family that once owned 50 acres (20.2 ha) of land and had a thousand dollars in the bank. Forever clinging to cleanliness, decency, and respectability, "There is still pride in the family," Steinbeck notes. "Wherever they stop they try to put the children in school. It may be that the children will be in school for as much as a month before they are moved to another locality."[11]

The second family, a clear step down, once owned a grocery store, but now lives in a tattered, rotten canvas tent. "There is no toilet here, but there is a clump of willows nearby where human feces lie exposed to the flies—the same flies that are in the tent," Steinbeck tells his readers. "A child, four-years-old, has recently died of fever and malnutrition."[12]

The third family occupies the lowest rung in the camp ladder. Their "house" consists of branches and scrap with no real walls or a roof. There is no bed, only a piece of old carpet lying on the ground. "To go to bed," Steinbeck says, "the members of the family lie on the ground and fold the carpet over them."[13]

Steinbeck makes it clear that soon enough, families in the first group will fall to the level of the second, and then, eventually, to the third. Such was the life awaiting those fleeing supposedly "worse" conditions in the Dust Bowl Great Plains of the 1930s Depression.

MIGRANT MOTHER

Words, powerful as they could be in the hands of a talented writer such as John Steinbeck, were not the only way in which Americans learned the plight of their fellow unemployed, underemployed, and poor citizens. Photographic images were, in some cases, an even more potent conveyer of the grinding poverty and hopelessness that the Depression had come to signify. Of all the photographers, from Ben Shahn, Margaret Bourke-White, Marion Post Walcott, Gordon Parks, and Russell Lee, who would in the end snap more than a quarter million pictures, Dorothea Lange stands out with her searing images of suffering farmers. Working for the California State Emergency Relief Administration (SERA), as well as the Farm Security Administration (FSA), Lange took what would turn out to be some of the most iconic, heart-wrenching images of destitution of the twentieth century.

Lange started out as a portrait photographer, taking pictures of the rich and famous in her San Francisco studio. As

Dorothea Lange's photograph "Migrant Mother" depicts a weary mother surrounded by her children. As one of the most iconic images of the twentieth century, this photograph successfully conveys the emotional and physical toll of the Great Depression.

the Depression deepened, however, she found it more difficult to continue such work. In 1933, she glanced out her studio window to see a breadline of unemployed and homeless men.

Grabbing a camera, she hurriedly snapped a photo. Later titled "White Angel Breadline," it became the first of thousands of Depression images she would eventually convey to the world.

Hired by the SERA, Lange left San Francisco to travel the Midwest and West, camera in hand. In her book, *Dorothea Lange: Archive of an Artist*, Karen Tsujimoto describes Lange as "Photographing what she saw—the cross section of migrant laborers ranging from white, Midwest-drought refugees to Mexicans and Filipinos, and the makeshift squatters' camps in which they lived, where shelters were sometimes made of only a few branches, rags, or palm leaves."[14]

Lange reported, "We found filth, squalor, an entire absence of sanitation, and a crowding of human beings into totally inadequate tents or crude structures built of boards, weeds, and anything that was found at hand to give a pitiful semblance of a home at its worst. Words cannot describe some of the conditions we saw."[15]

In March 1936, while returning home after a month on the road, the photographer spotted a sign reading "PEA PICKERS CAMP." In the camp, Lange found a 32-year-old woman, Florence Thompson, with three of her seven children huddled in a makeshift lean-to tent. The mother and children had been living on frozen vegetables from the surrounding fields and birds that the children had, with difficulty, managed to kill. The pea crop at Nipomo, California, had frozen, and there was no work for anyone.

It was here that Lange would take what would become, arguably, the most famous and widely reproduced photographic image of the twentieth century. Known as *Migrant Mother*, the photograph of Thompson (looking at least twenty years beyond her age) and the three children was the last of six shots Lange took. According to Mark Durden, in the famous image, "Lange removes background detail and hides the distracting countenances of the two children (who are literally pressing upon their mother, hemming her in) by getting them to bury their heads away from the camera. Focus is now on the expression on the mother's face, who in a moment of withdrawal, looks away from both photographer and children."[16]

Though there is little doubt that the photograph of Thompson was composed, the woman's plight was real enough. Throughout the land, in the mid-1930s, struggling as the New Deal was to succeed, millions of Americans still suffered mightily. Thanks to photographers such as Dorothea Lange, their story is there to see—in black and white.

Roosevelt's Radical Opponents

They called him a "traitor to his class," one who, though having been to the manor born, was now, in the eyes of the rich, no longer one of them. Franklin Delano Roosevelt had, with his New Deal legislation, discarded time-honored principles of conservative, market-oriented policies to take the country in a new, dangerous, "socialist" direction, the well-off lamented. To combat such radicalism and fend off the "tyrants" of the New Deal, a few prominent wealthy businessmen banded together on August 22, 1934, to form the American Liberty League. With the likes of Alfred E. Stone of General Motors, the Du Pont family, and conservative Democrats such as Al Smith and John Raskob, the league promised an "unremitting fight against government encroachments upon the rights of citizens."[1] Their main goal was to defeat Roosevelt in his bid for reelection in 1936.

The league, claiming 125,000 members by the summer of 1936 (the vast majority of whom were "rich-wannabes," not the actual rich), went on a campaign to restore to business the privileges it had enjoyed under Republican administrations of the 1920s. The league maintained that the New Deal not only restricted government recovery, but did so on purpose in order to sustain the economic crisis, and thus maintain Democrats in power. An unofficial whispering campaign charged Roosevelt, "with being a syphilitic, an alcoholic, a dictator, a dupe of blacks and Jews, and a pathological liar."[2]

A Roosevelt aide, responding to such slurs, declared of the American Liberty League, "It is like cellophane—first, it's a Du Pont product and second, you can see right through it."[3] For all its ranting and raving, for all the money it could contribute, the league had little effect on the presidential election of 1936. To most, FDR was not the problem—he was the solution. "Starving miners pasted newspaper pictures of Roosevelt on their curtainless windows. Factory girls wore Roosevelt buttons for jewelry. Intellectuals, farmers, Negroes, Jews, and educated women responded to his defense of human values against property rights."[4]

The class warfare inspiring the American Liberty League did nothing for the organization and the Republican Party's bid to regain the White House. Calling the American Liberty League "lovers of property," Roosevelt had little trouble painting its members and supporters as being in a "class by themselves." He would win the November election against Republican Alfred Landon in a landslide.

Opposition to Roosevelt and his liberal policies did not end with his reelection in 1936, however—far from it. With the coming to power of committed Fascists in European countries such as Italy, Germany, Austria, Spain, Romania, and Hungary in the decade of the 1930s, the appeal for government institutions that would supposedly operate more efficiently, and make the trains run on time, was powerful. In such corporate states, governments would work cooperatively with businesses and direct their operations. Curiously, despite the pro-labor, antibusiness accusations leveled against Roosevelt, many of the same individuals hurling such blame chose to see the president as a right-wing dictator in the mode of Benito Mussolini and even Adolf Hitler. Such was the political confusion of the times.

"FELLOW TRAVELERS"

On May 16, 1929, five months before the stock market crashed, the leader of the Soviet Union, Joseph Stalin, made a prediction. "I think the moment is not far off when a revolutionary crisis will develop in America," he said.[5] The head of the Communist Party in the United States (CP-USA), William Z. Foster, added to Stalin's remarks by declaring, "I see increasing militancy of the workers."[6] Indeed, in the early 1930s, as economic conditions deteriorated and citizens everywhere sought solutions outside the "box" of capitalism, things began looking up for American Communists. In 1929, the party had fewer than 10,000 members. By 1934, that number had jumped to 25,000. A half million more nonmembers, known as "Fellow Travelers," swelled the ranks even further. Figuratively, and even in some cases literally, the CP-USA was on the march.

Communist support was particularly strong in New York City, where "clubs" sprang up everywhere. In the Bronx, there were supposedly so many Communists that the area's CP-USA chairman, Isadore Begun, claimed that if he needed to convene a meeting, he only had to "knock on the steam pipe."

The Communists had their greatest success when infiltrating the U.S. labor movement. In the waterfront unrest of 1934, an Australian named Harry Bridges emerged as the strike's leader. He was accused of being a Communist. While it was not illegal to be a member of the Communist Party or run for office as a Communist, foreigners who had pledged to work for the overthrow of the capitalist system could be deported. Years after the waterfront strike, in 1945, Bridges became a

Interest in the Communist Party dramatically increased during the Great Depression, as growing numbers of unemployed workers became attracted to its political message. Above, 60,000 people staged a Communist demonstration in New York City on March 6, 1930.

U.S. citizen. When asked, "Are you now, or have you ever been, a Communist?" he answered "No, Your Honor." When the Kremlin archives were opened, after the fall of the Soviet Union in the early 1990s, it was verified that Bridges had indeed been a Communist agent, with the code name "Rossi."[7]

While often eager to support labor unrest for their own gain, the Communists scored a significant publicity triumph with their backing of the Scottsboro Boys, a case representing, arguably, the most celebrated instance of racial injustice in American history.

In late March 1931, a number of black men (actually boys ranging in age from 13 to 20) hopped a freight train traveling through Tennessee to look for work. According to Glenda Elizabeth Gilmore, in her book, *Defying Dixie*:

> Desperate people packed the train, hoboing around to find work, and fights broke out between black and white riders. The bloodied whites got off at Stevens, Alabama, and the stationmaster wired ahead to the next stop to "capture every negro on the train." As the train approached Paint Rock,

POPULAR FRONT

In 1935, Communist parties throughout the world, on a signal from Moscow, undertook a momentous shift. In the past, such parties, particularly in the United States, sought to oppose everything liberal and progressive, to place themselves in dead opposition to all social-democratic movements, even going so far as to disrupt their meetings and block their programs. Communists eagerly developed parallel unions that competed with existing unions. But with the coming of what would now be called the Popular Front all that changed. In an attempt to combat European Fascism, all Communist parties were instructed to join with "progressive" forces in fighting the common Fascist enemy. Communists now made common cause with Socialists and liberals, and even gave qualified support for many New Deal programs and to President Roosevelt himself.

a few of the black riders saw an angry crowd waiting and jumped off before the train pulled into the station. A mob of over two hundred whites met the train, searched it, and discovered nine black teenagers, who had been scattered in different cars."[8]

They also spotted two white women, Ruby Bates and Victoria Price, dressed in men's clothing. Both would claim they had been raped by some of the black men on the train. As a result, the nine black youths arrested would spend the better part of the thirties, and beyond, in Alabama prisons, suffering nightmare rounds of convictions, appeals, and reconvictions. The Communist International Labor Defense retained Samuel

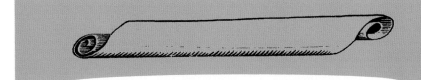

The message of the Popular Front was of unity and interdependence, of diversity and community. Their motif was the handshake, one that signified mutual recognition across barriers of class and race. All left-leaning individuals, groups, and institutions were to unite in "brotherly love."

All this ended, however, when, in August 1939, Stalin and Hitler signed a nonaggression pact. Now the Communist Party saw the European war as an "imperialist" war, caused by Great Britain and France. Communist-dominated unions were quick to go out on strike. Yet when Germany attacked Russia, in June of 1941, it was time for the Communist Party to flip again. Now "imperialist" became "democratic." Strikes were prohibited, being a hindrance to the war effort. In 1944, the U.S. Communist Party "disbanded" and became known as the Communist Political Association. Today it is recognized as Communist Party USA.

S. Leibowitz to defend the blacks. Despite a vigorous defense, the boys would remain in jail, in some cases, for decades.

Though the Communists gained considerable respect with their actions in the Scottsboro case, their power to influence the wider political processes of the 1930s never gained traction. Their impact would wane significantly in the decades to follow.

THREE VOICES

While Americans vacillated back and forth from the political right to the political left in seeking answers to the economic distress the Great Depression had visited upon them, three striking individuals (with personalities and crackpot schemes to garner widespread attention) enlivened the political debate. Dr. Francis Townsend, Father Charles Coughlin, and Senator Huey Long would give the public plenty to ponder with their alternatives to the Roosevelt New Deal.

Francis Townsend

The gentlest of the three, Dr. Townsend, a retired physician living in Long Beach, California, hit upon a bold scheme that he felt would save retirees and at the same time draw the country out of the Depression. One morning while the good doctor was shaving, he glanced out the window to see three old women scrounging through garbage cans for bits of food. Shocked and outraged, Townsend came up with a plan he called the Old Age Revolving Pension. In short order, millions of Americans would be eagerly backing the "Townsend Plan."

What Dr. Townsend proposed would call for a guaranteed monthly pension of $200 to be given to retired citizens over the age of 60. (In the 1930s, $200 a month would put a family squarely in the middle class.) The money would come from a national sales tax of 2 percent on all business transactions. Individuals receiving the pension would be required to spend every penny of their $200 gift within 30 days. By doing this, Townsend and his supporters argued, the country would work its way out of poverty, aided by the consumer spending of the older generation. As a bonus, the doctor was quick to point out, older folks would be removed from the labor market.

Townsend clubs sprang up all over America. By the end of 1935, 7,000 existed, with a combined membership of at least 2.2 million.[9] A *Townsend National Weekly* was published. Townsend buttons, stickers, tire covers, and automobile plates proliferated. At rallies Townsendites rose to sing:

Onward, Townsend soldiers,
Marching as to war,
With the Townsend banner
Going on before.
Our devoted soldiers
Bid depression go;
Join them in the battle,
Help them fight the foe![10]

In the end, the scheme proved unworkable. It was estimated that the tax needed to generate the required pension money would account for almost half the national income. Nonetheless, the Townsend Plan had an enormous influence on New Deal planners. Clearly, it spurred Secretary of Labor Frances Perkins in her efforts to create Social Security, an old-age pension the government and the country could live with.

Father Charles Coughlin

Although the 1930s were synonymous with the Depression, the decade was also known for being "the Golden Age of Radio." The two were clearly linked.

For millions of Americans, most of whom could little afford more expensive, "going out" entertainments, the radio proved a godsend. In some cases, for less than $8, a cheap "talking box" could be placed in the home as a table model. Nicer radios ran to $50. And for a mahogany and rosewood Stromberg-Carlson console, the size of a bedroom bureau, the price skyrocketed to $500—a third the annual wage of a workingman, assuming he was working.

As a source of entertainment and information, the radio had an amazing ability to pull listeners in. Starting in the early 1930s, Americans got plenty of both while tuned to one of the era's most remarkable personalities—the "radio priest," Father Charles E. Coughlin. Based in Royal Oaks, Michigan, at the Shrine of the Little Flower Church, Coughlin, an ordained priest, would soon find himself, thanks to radio, projecting his fiery anticapitalist and anticommunist sermons far beyond his home base. At the height of his popularity, it was said that 40 million people, a third of the nation, were taking in his Sunday broadcasts. Coughlin received 80,000 letters a week from listeners, more than the president. In 1934, *Fortune* magazine said Coughlin was "just about the biggest thing that ever happened to radio."[11]

Coughlin was at first a vigorous champion of Franklin Roosevelt. In the election of 1932, the priest claimed that the choice was "Roosevelt or ruin."[12] In January of 1934, Coughlin testified before Congress in support of FDR's polices, saying, "If Congress fails to back up the president in his monetary program, I predict a revolution in this country which will make the French Revolution look silly! God is directing President Roosevelt."[13] By the end of the year, however, Coughlin would turn on the president for failing to enact a "free silver" fiscal policy, denouncing him as a dictator.

Coughlin was a curious demagogue, able to denounce capitalist "money changers" in one radio broadcast and Communists in another. In 1935, Father Coughlin declared, "I have dedicated my life to fight against the heinous rottenness of modern capitalism because it robs the laborer of this world's goods. But blow for blow, I shall strike against Communism, because it robs us of the next world's happiness."[14]

In the end, after calling the president a liar, Coughlin became estranged from the Catholic Church. Though he lived to see his eighty-eighth birthday, with the coming of World War II his influence evaporated. Radio would not see the likes of such a rabble-rouser for another half century.

Huey Long

Francis Townsend and Charles Coughlin, though popular and influential, never held public office. The third man in the nation's triumvirate of demagogues, however, most certainly did. He was governor of and senator from Louisiana, and for more than a year, both at the same time. Huey Long, known affectionately as the Kingfish, was, indeed, quite a politician. Fiercely smart, persuasively eloquent, and notoriously unscrupulous, he was a man with towering ambition who was unfettered by self-doubt. The time would come when the Roosevelt administration would consider the log-cabin born "owner of Louisiana" a serious rival for president.

Huey Long was convinced that the uneven distribution of wealth had caused the Great Depression. At the time, while technically both a Louisiana governor and senator, Long came up with a "share the wealth" plan that though economically unattainable, was politically powerful. Under his program, every family in the nation would be guaranteed:

☆ An annual income of $2,000 to $3,000
☆ A 30-hour work week
☆ An annual one-month vacation
☆ Old-age pensions
☆ Free college for "deserving" students
☆ Government purchase of farm surpluses[15]

In April 1935, Long's Senate office received 60,000 letters of support. More than 27,000 "Share Our Wealth" clubs were

Although not an ideal candidate for president, Senator Huey Long from Louisiana was one of the greatest threats to President Roosevelt's presidency. Long was assassinated just as he was beginning to gather support for a presidential campaign.

formed. The organization claimed to have at least 4.6 million members.[16]

In short order, Long's delightful followers began singing a song Long wrote himself:

> *Every man a king, every girl a queen,*
> *For you can be a millionaire,*
> *But there's something belonging to others,*
> *There's enough for all people to share.*
> *In sunny June and December too,*
> *In the winter time and spring*
> *There'll be peace without end,*
> *Every neighbor a friend*
> *With every man a king.*[17]

Though, like Father Coughlin, Huey Long was initially a supporter of Roosevelt, by early 1935 the Kingfish was laying plans to replace FDR in the White House. In truth, however, Long was simply too parochial, too vulgar to be a serious presidential candidate. "He threw food on a restaurant floor when it wasn't cooked to his taste, kept his hat on throughout an interview with President Roosevelt, and at the Sands Point Club on Long Island committed a nuisance on another guest's trouser leg when the gentleman was slow to yield Huey a place at the urinal," wrote Robert Bendiner. "The last of these episodes became rather well publicized and almost undermined his standing, because the guest in question punched him enthusiastically, leaving a deep cut above the eye to advertise the conquest."[18]

On the evening of September 8, 1935, while in his home state checking up on the governor he had handpicked to replace him, Long, along with bodyguards, was seen making his way through the capital building. A slender, bespectacled man emerged from behind a column with a small pistol in hand. He fired one shot, hitting the senator. In response, the bodyguards opened up on Dr. Carl Austin Weiss, the assassin, riddling his body with 61 bullets and killing him. To this day, speculation remains as to whether the whole thing was a setup by Long's enemies to enlist the bodyguards in the deadly scheme. Long died 30 hours later.

Long's elimination from the national scene removed Roosevelt's greatest political nightmare. Yet Francis Townsend's plan to give every senior citizen a comfortable pension, Charles Coughlin's scheme to bring down men of greed and wealth, and Huey Long's promises to create a society where "every man is a king but no man wears a crown," would continue to attract supporters and admirers. Seven years after the stock market crash of 1929, the Great Depression that it fostered was still far from over.

National Pastimes

The Great Depression slowed down just about everything and everyone. At least it did at first, during the administration of Herbert Hoover, from 1929 to early 1933. But with the coming of Franklin Delano Roosevelt and his New Deal, there sprang an optimism, a hope for the future that propelled countless Americans to get up, get out, pull together, and make things happen—to, above all, make their lives and their world move! Referring to everything from popular big bands to streamlined consumer products, Morris Dickstein declared, "All these offered wit, energy, class, style, and movement (above all, movement) to people whose lives were stagnant, fearful, deprived of hope, people who often took to the road but rarely had anywhere to go."[1]

In the arts, what would come to be known as Art Deco, but at the time was usually referred to as Depression Modern, took hold to reflect this movement, this get-up-and-go that the country so desperately sought and needed. Though "born" in Europe, at the great Paris Art Exhibition of 1925, Art Deco sprang to full fruition in the United States during the 1930s. Begun as a "smart" urban style among a small contingent of upper-middle-class elitists in Chicago and New York, Art Deco soon spread to the common culture, first in the form of major architectural structures, then, in the latter part of the decade, to mass-produced machine products and consumer goods. Its fundamental characteristic, consisting of distinct geometric shapes, intense bright colors, and angular composition empha- sizing the vertical, was meant to perk up lagging consumer demand during the Depression. It may well have done the trick.

Architecturally, three structures in particular, all within a few blocks of each other in midtown Manhattan, rose up between 1928 and 1933 to display, in all their grandeur, every- thing that Art Deco could be. The Chrysler Building, with its distinctive ornamental "automotive" eagle gargoyles (repre- senting hood ornaments) and a massive stainless steel, seven- layered dome, was the first to be completed. Soon to follow, to rise the highest of all, would be the Empire State Building. And not to be outdone in demonstrating a profound faith in New York's and the nation's future, the 11.7-acre (4.7 ha) Rockefeller Center, with its Radio City Music Hall, took center stage in quick order. Hundreds of such buildings, albeit on a far more modest scale, would dot Manhattan in the next few years. It would not stop there, of course. By decade's end, prac- tically every city in America was displaying the Art Deco motif in one form or another.

It was not just buildings that went Art Deco either. Every product imaginable, from sleek locomotives, to farm equip- ment, to a household iron, pencil sharpener, or cigarette lighter took on the Art Deco look, one of sleek, modern, graceful flow—of streamlining. "Art Deco," Dickstein pointed out, "didn't create any new products as such, but it made familiar

The Great Depression spurred many of America's greatest building projects, including the Empire State Building. Above, a steel worker rests on the eighty-sixth floor of the Empire State Building with the Chrysler Building behind him.

things look new and provoked a hunger for more new-looking things that it was happy to keep feeding."[2]

"New" meant more spending. More spending meant more jobs. More jobs meant economic growth. The ensuing expanding economy meant better tomorrows.

DANCING IN THE DARK

On May 3, 1903, six-year-old Harry Lillis Crosby, the fourth of seven children, on, picked up an unusual nickname from an older schoolmate: Bing, from "Bingo." He would grow up to become one of the greatest entertainers of the twentieth century.

Bing Crosby got his start, as did many young singers after him, while playing in a school band. In college, he sent away for a set of mail-order drums. Bing became so good at playing them, he was invited to join in The Musicaladers, a band managed by Al Rinker. The "drummer boy" made so much money doing regional gigs that in 1920 he dropped out of school in his final year to pursue a career in show business. He never looked back.

JUST SING

In an attempt to brighten spirits and give hope to millions, songwriters of the 1930s wrote many memorable lyrics. Two songs, in particular, stand out: "Pennies from Heaven," and "Wrap Your Troubles in Dreams." Excerpts of lyrics from both are as follows:

"Pennies From Heaven"
Every time it rains it rains
Pennies from heaven.
Don't you know each cloud contains
Pennies from heaven.
You'll find your fortune falling
All over town.
Be sure that your umbrella is upside down.
Trade them for a package of sunshine and flowers.
If you want the things you love
You must have showers.

In 1928, Crosby joined "The King of Jazz," Paul Whiteman, probably the most famous bandleader at the time. The twenty-five-year-old singer immediately became a huge success. By 1931, 10 of the top 50 songs recorded featured Crosby solo or with others. A key to the crooner's achievement was his perfection in the use of the microphone, an instrument that allowed a singer to "converse" rather than belt. Between 1934 and 1954, Bing Crosby would go on to become the undisputed best-selling artist ever. At one time, more than half of the 80,000 weekly hours allocated to recorded radio music belonged to Crosby. He made more than 1,700 recordings, 383 of those in

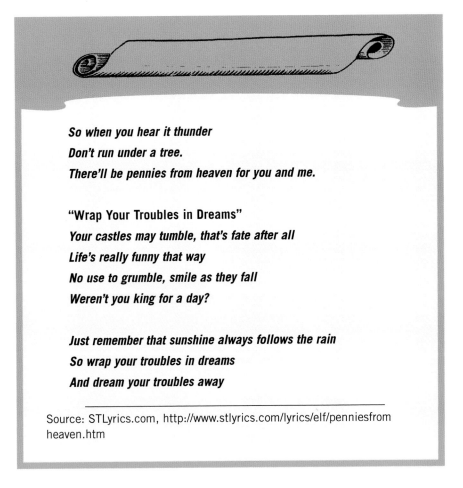

So when you hear it thunder
Don't run under a tree.
There'll be pennies from heaven for you and me.

"Wrap Your Troubles in Dreams"
Your castles may tumble, that's fate after all
Life's really funny that way
No use to grumble, smile as they fall
Weren't you king for a day?

Just remember that sunshine always follows the rain
So wrap your troubles in dreams
And dream your troubles away

Source: STLyrics.com, http://www.stlyrics.com/lyrics/elf/penniesfrom heaven.htm

the top 30, and of those, 41 rose to number one. During his life-time, Crosby sold more than half a billion records. His "White Christmas" has, to date, sold more than 100 million copies—making it the best-selling song of all time.[3]

Crosby's voice was, according to Louis Armstrong, "like gold poured out of a cup."[4] To a vast audience, Crosby was the essence of cool. He was also a singer for his time, one who would continually, throughout the 1930s, put out overt Depression material.

One of Crosby's most notable recordings was of a song written by Arthur Schwartz and Howard Dietz, called *Dancing in the Dark* (1931). Crosby's version of the song goes beyond the dance floor to, as Morris Dickstein noted, "Evoke a sense of the darkness surrounding our lives."[5] It spoke to the ongoing troubles of the Great Depression.

> *Dancing in the dark, till the tune ends,*
> *We're dancing in the dark and it soon ends,*
> *We're waltzing in the wonder of why we're here,*
> *Time hurries by, we're here . . . and gone;*
>
> *Looking for the light of a new love,*
> *To brighten up the night, I have you love,*
> *And we can face the music together,*
> *Dancing in the dark.*[6]

To Dickstein, "The range of emotion that Crosby brought to this song, the mixture of melancholy and hope, could not have been better keyed to the moment. . . . The idea that 'we can face the music together' became a keystone of the New Deal."[7]

TAKING A GAMBLE

If, during the Depression, Americans found their lives slow-ing down, they also saw the time in their lives stretching out. Most had more of it than they knew what to do with. Killing time became a major issue, an important pastime. According to a National Recreation Association survey of 1934, Americans spent time in solitary, sedentary, and spectatorial activities, though what they really wanted to do was go somewhere, make something, or just do something. "People told the investigators they had given up outside group activities because they had 'no money for carfare' and 'no proper clothes' or were 'too discouraged or worried because of loss of job to concentrate on anything.'"[8] Many were simply too embarrassed to be seen in public.

The number one leisure-time activity for most people was reading, either newspapers or magazines. Listening to the radio was number two, followed by going to the movies. What people most wanted to do, however, was, first, play tennis, followed by swimming, and then boating. In other words, they longed to do what they thought the rich had the time and money to engage in.

What Americans did find time for, regardless of what they had to wear or how they would get to the point of engagement, was gambling. Invented in 1895, the slot machine was reintroduced to the public in the 1930s with major innovations, making it a Depression phenomenon. The double jackpot, which assured players that one could win twice in quick succession, sucked in the suckers. The appeal was hypnotic. "It didn't matter that the machine was rigged to keep from 20 to 70 percent of all coins put into it," wrote Caroline Bird. "It didn't matter that half the take went into organized crime, which had moved in on the slots after Prohibition was repealed. What mattered was the anesthetic of the whir, punctuated by the momentary thrill of getting something for nothing. By the time Pearl Harbor [1941] produced some real excitement, the slots were gobbling up more than ten times as much change as they had taken at the time of the 1929 Crash."[9]

When pari-mutuel betting, a pool-based gambling system, on horse racing became legal in 1934, receipts at racetracks around the country tripled. It was not just the money that drew people to the races, however; it was also the star power of the horses themselves, with one in particular a supernova all his own. "In 1938, near the end of a decade of monumental turmoil, the year's number-one newsmaker was not Franklin Delano Roosevelt, Hitler, or Mussolini," wrote author Laura Hillenbrand. "It wasn't Pope Pius XI, nor was it Lou Gehrig, Howard Hughes, or Clark Gable. The subject of the most newspaper column inches in 1938 wasn't even a person. It was an undersized, crooked-legged racehorse named Seabiscuit."[10]

Thus did Americans seek escape from their troubles, from the relentless economically depressing conditions all around them. Though, with the reelection of Franklin D. Roosevelt in 1936, and the launch of the second New Deal, unemployment did decrease, nonetheless, far too many citizens were still in no mood to return to old spending habits. Money was tight and time was heavy. For the vast majority, the duration had to be filled as cheaply as possible.

GANGSTER DOINGS

With the repeal of Prohibition in 1933, the gangster underclass, represented by the likes of George "Machine Gun" Kelley, Charles "Lucky" Luciano, and Benjamin "Bugsy" Siegel shifted operations, notably to gambling. There was big money to be made on "the numbers," the turn of a card, the roll of the dice, and the whirl of a roulette wheel. Lucky Luciano took the lead in such efforts, forming, in 1934, the infamous La Cosa Nostra ("our thing") crime racket to control operations on a national scale. Of course, gambling was not the only vice on a list of illegal "enterprises" to be engaged in—organized prostitution, extortion, and racketeering were also in the mix.

More traditional ways of making an illegal buck did not disappear with the rise of organized crime. Indeed, with the advent of fast cars and the acquisition of machine guns, bank robbing became all that much easier. In 1933, such robberies were being pulled at a rate of two a day. "Not since the Wild

West era of Jesse James, the Dalton Brothers, and Butch Cassidy and the Sundance Kid had Americans witnessed such a blizzard of brazen bank holdups," wrote Paul Jeffers. "But now the daredevil escapes were made in automobiles that sped the crooks safely out of reach of local cops by crossing state lines."[11]

To combat the easy escape route across state borders, Congress passed a measure that allowed federal government agents to go after anyone who crossed state lines to avoid prosecution. The Justice Department's Bureau of Investigation, later named the Federal Bureau of Investigation (FBI), was given the job of rounding up fleeing criminals. With the appointment of J. (John) Edgar Hoover as the agency's director, in 1924, the bad guys met their match. When Hoover's "G-Men" (government men) busted in on George Kelly, holed up in a house in Memphis, Tennessee, on the night of September 25, 1933, their reputation was sealed. G-Men would forever become part of America's crime control.

One did not have to be part of an organized crime ring to make it big (at least in the public's eye) when it came to robbery and mayhem. Bonnie and Clyde, a pair of Texas misfits, filled the bill nicely, speeding around the country holding up banks, stealing a hundred dollars here, another hundred there. The pair became folk heroes because they were seen as taking from institutions (banks) that had "stolen" from farmers and other down-and-out, law-abiding Americans struggling to survive the Depression. Of course, there was little doubt that the couple would meet a bad end. A song written about the pair went:

> *Some day they will go down together,*
> *And they will bury them side by side.*
> *To a few it means grief.*
> *To the law it's a relief.*
> *But it's death to Bonnie and Clyde.*[12]

The finale did come, in a police ambush, on May 23, 1934.

Bonnie and Clyde became household names as they drove throughout the country, robbed banks, and eluded capture. Although they were armed and dangerous, their love story and lawlessness captured the attention of the nation.

AMELIA EARHART

Though the tough guys of the 1930s did bad things, they were seen by many as heroes, not only because of their supposed "Robin Hood" personas of stealing from those who had, but, in a distorted way, because they were successful businessmen and/or entrepreneurs. Down-and-out, either because of difficult times or for having been born into poverty, many rose to take command of their lives, short-lived as they may have been—something almost everyone at the time aspired to do. For a true hero, or heroine, Americans of the Depression decade did not need to turn to the likes of criminals, however. The decade produced many men and women of outstanding qualities. One, in particular, was the pilot Amelia Earhart, who captured the minds and hearts of countless citizens longing for someone good and noble to believe in.

Born in Atchison, Kansas, on July 24, 1897, Amelia grew up a true tomboy. In 1904, she, along with her uncle, cobbled together a homemade ramp and secured it to the roof of the family toolshed. Amelia's "first flight" ended rather dramatically. She emerged from the crushed wooden box used as a sled with a torn dress and a bruised lip. Unfazed, the feisty gal told her sister, Pidge, "Why, it's just like flying."[13]

It was not, however, until 1920 that Earhart actually flew. While visiting an airfield in Long Beach, California, with her father, Earhart took to the air for a 10-minute flight. "By the time I had got two or three hundred feet [61 to 91 meters] off the ground," she declared, "I knew I had to fly."[14]

The rest is history. Earhart became the first woman to fly the Atlantic, albeit as a passenger, in 1928. Four years later, however, she accomplished the feat solo—the first woman to do so. Landing in Derry, Northern Ireland, a farmhand asked Amelia, "Have you flown far?" The aviatrix replied, "From America."[15]

The following year, Earhart became the first woman to fly nonstop, coast to coast, across the United States. By then,

Amelia Earhart, tall, slender, and blonde, had become a national icon, adored for her daring and spunk—two human qualities longed for and admired during the economic troubles besetting the nation.

On July 2, 1937, Earhart and her navigator, Fred Noonan, took off from Lae, New Guinea, on the last leg of what would have been an around-the-world flight. Flying a Lockheed twin-engine L-10E Electra, the pair were heading east, to Howland Island, about halfway between New Guinea and Hawaii. They never made it.

What happened to Amelia Earhart and her navigator has been the cause of intense speculation and investigation to this day. One enticing, though improbable, theory is that the two made a forced landing on Nikumaroro Island, a tiny coral atoll, some 300 miles (482 km) southeast of their target destination. They became castaways and eventually died there.

The loss of Amelia Earhart stunned the nation. And it came at a particularly bad time. In 1937, the economy, having shown genuine progress during the past couple of years, seemed to be slipping back, with unemployment rising again. The Japanese had invaded Manchuria the previous year, setting up a brutal occupation. And in Europe, Mussolini and Hitler were becoming more threatening every day. Hard times, bad times; Americans wondered when they would ever end.

World War II
and the
Depression's End

In the year that Amelia Earhart vanished, perhaps into the clouds over the vast, lonely Pacific, America saw plenty of clouds, looming on its horizon as well. Would this Great Depression, one that had kept millions of people, rural and urban, in what seemed a perpetual state of poverty for the last eight years, ever cease to be? Would the country, the economy, ever return to a "normal" business cycle? Would the long-lasting bust ever again reverse and turn into a long-sought boom?

In terms of the U.S. gross domestic product (GDP), in current dollars, the country had gone from a pre-crash 1929 figure of $103.6 billion to $56.4 billion in 1933, the year Herbert Hoover's presidency ended. By 1937, it had clawed back to $91.9 billion, 88 percent of the previous value. The economic recovery of 1933 to 1937, which saw double-digit annual gains, was among the most dramatic in U.S. history. Yet, in 1938, as a result of a tax increase and the reduction in government spending, the GDP took a dip, down to $86.1 billion.[1] A recession within the Depression had materialized.

The Dow Jones Industrial Average, which stood at 381.7 points in September 1929, fell to 41.22 in July of 1932, losing 90 percent of its value. It would not reach a figure higher than the 1929 peak until November of 1954, a quarter of a century after the great crash.[2]

Unemployment, the most important indicator of economic health, remained, except in 1930, in double digits throughout the 1930s. In 1929, it stood at just 3.2 percent; everyone who wanted a job seemed to have one. In 1930, the number of people out of work hit 8.9 percent. When Franklin D. Roosevelt took office in 1933 the percentage peaked at 24.9, closer to 33 percent if the current definition of unemployment, which takes into account, among other things, those who have given up looking for work, is used. By 1937, unemployment had fallen to 14.23 percent. But in 1938, amid the Roosevelt recession, it was back up—to 19 percent.[3] Clearly, the New Deal helped to reduce unemployment from 1933 through 1937. But now, the year that Seabiscuit enthralled the nation, it seemed to be moving in the wrong direction again.

Internationally, dark clouds of a different kind were forming everywhere. In March 1938, Hitler annexed Austria. In the next couple of years, the Führer would march his German army all over Europe, encountering minimal resistance. In the Far East, Japan, too, was on the move. By 1937, it had conquered large swaths of China, engaging in unspeakable atrocities.

The United States was woefully unprepared to take on either of these adversaries, assuming it even wanted to. In 1938, the country had fewer than 2,000 planes, most of them obsolete. It had but 1,650 trained pilots. Germany, on the other hand, possessed 8,000 fighters and bombers in a rapidly expanding air force. Some of those German bombers, it was determined, could reach the United States.[4] The American

Hitler shocked the world when he led his troops into Vienna and annexed Austria. Although many were concerned about Hitler's aggression, the United States was still recovering from the Great Depression and tried to remain neutral.

army was in even poorer shape. By the end of the decade, it ranked only eighteenth in the world in size, behind Germany, France, Britain, Russia, Italy, Sweden, and even Switzerland.[5]

Economic struggles at home, a hostile world building abroad—Americans in the late 1930s had much to be apprehensive about.

WANING NEUTRALITY

Although President Roosevelt knew war was coming, and that the United States could not avoid involvement, the country was strongly isolationist in 1937. Late in the year, Congress attempted to renew the Neutrality Act of 1935, with the belief that by denying the government the capacity to make war it was somehow securing the peace. Polls showed 73 percent of the American people supporting the act.[6] It was defeated only after extensive lobbying by the White House.

Speaking directly to the isolationists, Roosevelt declared:

> If those things [international conflict] come to pass in other parts of the world, let no one imagine that America will escape, that America may expect mercy, that this Western hemisphere will not be attacked and that it will continue tranquilly and peacefully to carry on the ethics and the arts of civilization. If those days come, there will be no safety by arms, no help from authority, no answer in science. The storm will rage till every flower of culture is trampled and all human beings are leveled in a vast chaos. . . . There is no escape through mere isolation or neutrality.[7]

It was a tough sell. Twenty years earlier, President Woodrow Wilson told Americans they needed to aid Europe in its struggles against tyranny because doing so would create a world in which the strong no longer menaced the weak. But when war ended, and the victorious European powers, according to Peter Beinart,

WORLD'S FAIRS

Building on a long and successful tradition, in the 1930s, Americans saw the creation of two giant world's fairs, both designed to mitigate the effects of the ongoing Great Depression.

The first fair, known as the Century of Progress Exposition, was built in Chicago, on a 400-acre (161.8 ha) landfill on the edge of Lake Michigan. According to the fair's president, Rufus C. Dawes, the exposition's purpose was to show the world "the spontaneous expression of pride of citizenship of Chicago." The fair ran for 19 months. Indeed, by the time the fair closed on October 31, 1934, 38 million people took in the Windy City's glories as it celebrated its hundredth anniversary.

Five years later, a second, far more ambitious world's fair opened in New York. Also built on a dump site, the 1939 fair, dubbed as the World of Tomorrow, featured the Perisphere and Trylon as its centerpiece. On August 26, 1939, its single busiest day, 306,408 people attended. Forty-five million would eventually see the fair, with adults being charged 75¢ to get in, while kids under 14 paid a quarter.

The Perisphere contained an exhibit called Democracity. According to Paul H. Jeffers:

> This was a diorama depicting a future idyllic city and countryside. Inside a space as large as Radio City Music Hall, fair-goers were transported on two "magic carpets" (revolving platforms) to gaze in wonder, as the advertising said, "as if from Olympian heights to pierce the fogs of ignorance, habit, and prejudice that envelope everyday thinking, and gaze down on the ideal community that man could build today were he to make full use of his tools, his resources, and his knowledge."

Source: Jeffers, Paul H. *The Complete Idiot's Guide to the Great Depression*. New York: Penguin Group, 2002 p. 287.

writing in *Time*, "had no interest in birthing such a world,"[8] Americans said no to any further continental involvement.

Wilson's failure haunted Roosevelt. "His basic problem as Nazism stalked Europe was that some Americans wanted to isolate themselves from the world while others wanted to remake it in America's image," Beinart observed. "The U.S. could neither escape the world nor fully redeem it. FDR's task was to persuade his people to put their money and blood on the line, even though, despite their best efforts, the world would remain a nasty place."[9]

In no small part, due to the continued "bombardment" of photographs and newsreels documenting the harshness of German occupation as the Nazis stormed across Europe, American public opinion began to shift. By 1939, 60 percent of Americans favored repeal of the Neutrality Act.[10] At the end of September, Roosevelt called Congress into special session. On November 3, both the Senate and the House voted to repeal the old Neutrality Act. While some restrictions remained, under the Neutrality Act of 1939 America could sell arms and grant credits for arms purchases to nations at war. The United States could now start arming the Allies. Significantly, a lot of Americans would be put to work in doing so.

ARSENAL OF DEMOCRACY

In November 1938, President Roosevelt, talking privately with his secretary of the treasury, Henry Morgenthau, discussed the benefits of the world's slide into war, not only for America but for the Democratic Party. "These foreign orders for armaments, the president said, "mean prosperity in this country and we can't elect a Democratic Party unless we get prosperity."[11] While his party did lose seats in the midterm election of 1938, it still stayed in control of Congress. And, in 1940, Roosevelt won an unprecedented third term.

By May of 1940, the German army, in full *blitzkrieg* (lightning war) mode, moved ever onward in its goal of taking all of continental Europe. On June 4, after Britain's humiliating retreat at Dunkirk, Prime Minster Winston Churchill declared, "We shall go on to the end. We shall fight in the seas and oceans, we shall fight . . . in the air. We shall fight on the beaches, we shall fight on the landing grounds, we shall fight in the fields and in the streets, we shall fight in the hills; we shall never surrender."[12] In response, American public opinion shifted toward aiding the British. Roosevelt immediately ordered that enough rifles, artillery, machine guns, ammunition, and explosives be sent to replace those left behind at Dunkirk.

In December of 1940, Roosevelt, in a fireside chat, declared, "We must be the arsenal of democracy."[13] The aid the president was to offer became known as Lend-Lease. Passed into law in March of 1941, the program was a clever way in which the United States would supply war materiel to the British, either by sale, transfer, exchange, or lease. FDR exhorted Americans to help churn out "more ships, more guns, more planes—more of everything."[14] No one expected there would be any pressure to repay the "loan." Eventually totaling more than $50 billion, Churchill called Lend-Lease "the most unselfish act by one nation to help another in the history of the world."[15]

With factories humming to fill England's orders, unemployment in America began to fall significantly, down to 14.6 percent by the end of 1940.[16] Workers were in demand everywhere, to do almost everything. Housing was needed for defense workers in East Hartford, Connecticut, for example. A private contractor was given the job, one that would eventually employ 11,000 carpenters among a workforce of 20,000 men. "Crews working three shifts around the clock built Camp Edwards using production line methods, finishing 1,200 buildings in 125 days," noted Nick Taylor. "The first of 25,000 trainees began arriving in January 1941."[17]

War production continued to drive unemployment further down, something the New Deal itself had struggled, often with mixed success, to do for eight years. In 1941, it dropped below

10 percent—the first time since 1929 that it reached single digits. The number of jobless had fallen to 5.3 million, down from 13 to 15 million when Roosevelt took office.[18] And all of this occurred before the real mobilization of manpower began, with the need to enlist American men in the war's actually fighting.

AMERICA GOES TO WAR

On Sunday, December 7, 1941, Frances Perkins and all of President Roosevelt's cabinet ministers were called to an emergency meeting at the White House, scheduled for 8:00 P.M. Vice President Henry Wallace was summoned, too. An aide taking the secretary of labor to the White House informed her that Japan was "shooting at American ships. They've been dropping bombs on them. It happened in Honolulu."[19]

As the president's cabinet assembled, a naval officer told them that a Japanese fleet had bombed Pearl Harbor that morning. Many had died and many ships were lost. That was all that was known for now. According to Kirstin Downey, Perkins, only days earlier, had wondered whether the United States would send more aid to the British. She now wondered if the British would need to provide aid for the Americans.[20]

At about 9:00 P.M., the president, looking tired and gray, presented to his cabinet a declaration of war. No one questioned the decision. Perkins, however, felt the president's behavior was off. She was not prepared to admit that Roosevelt was playing a "false role," that he had prior knowledge of the situation in Hawaii. But, as she recorded in her notes later that evening, she was convinced that "his surprise was not as great as the surprise of the rest of us."[21]

No one will ever know what prior knowledge, if any, Roosevelt had about the Japanese surprise attack on American naval forces in the Pacific. What is fairly well accepted, however, is that FDR was probably glad the waiting was over, that he could now take action. Finally, the United States would join the fighting.

Above, President Roosevelt signs the declaration of war against the Axis powers in 1941 while surrounded by members of Congress and the Senate. The Japanese attack on Pearl Harbor forced the United States to enter World War II, an inevitable event that would put an end to the Great Depression.

The war, to be sure, proved to be an enormous economic stimulus. In 1942, the government spent $20 billion more than it collected to supply the arms and ammunition needed to fight both the Germans and the Japanese. As a direct result, unemployment fell below 5 percent. In 1943, everyone who could possibly work was working. Unemployment was, in reality, nonexistent, at a mere 2 percent. The national deficit, in the meantime, had climbed to $50 billion.

The government was now buying more goods and services than the entire economy had produced in any year of the 1930s.

So desperate for labor were the corporations of America, in order to attract talented workers in a time of wage freezes, many companies began offering their employees an unprecedented benefit—health insurance. For the American labor force, for the country as a whole, the Great Depression was at last over.

Conservative critics of the Roosevelt administration and his New Deal policies are quick to point out that it was not the New Deal that ended the Depression, it was World War II. Technically they are right, but they also miss a critical point. From an economic stimulus perspective, World War II was the New Deal writ large. If the New Deal was government spending on projects that put people to work, World War II magnified such efforts many times over. All that spending for Lend-Lease material and preparation at home put money in people's pockets and increased their spending, which, in turn, put even more people to work. Moreover, men who were not hired to build airplanes were "hired" to fly them. Between 1941 and 1945, 10 million joined the military as GIs (government issues).

Though World War II was a necessity, not an effort in economic recovery, that it improved the economy was a bonus all gladly accepted.

SOMEWHERE OVER THE RAINBOW

In looking back from the perspective of today, it is easy to see the Great Depression as having three phases. During the first phase, in the Hoover years from 1929 to 1933, the falling and failing economy drove Americans to the brink of despair. Although a caring man at heart, with vast experience in the distribution of government relief, Hoover simply could not get past his own considerable personal financial success and belief in rugged individualism to provide the direct federal aid necessary to pull the country out of its worst economic crisis in American history. Curiously, conservative historians would come to blame Hoover for going too far in providing government assistance, for not giving market forces time to work their "magic." Liberals simply scoffed at such a notion.

In the second phase of the Depression, during Roosevelt's first term, 1933 to 1937, the New Deal, with its "First Hundred Days" of heightened government legislation, gave Americans hope that the man in the White House was, above all, doing something. Not all the New Deal programs worked, not all of them provided the kind of relief and stimulation hoped for. But they did put people to work—millions of them. And, perhaps in an even more significant way, they pulled people together. Referring to the WPA, the premier New Deal effort at work relief, Nick Taylor concluded, "These ordinary men and women proved to be extraordinary beyond all expectations. . . . In this they shamed the political philosophy that discounted their value and rewarded the one that placed faith in them, thus fulfilling the founding vision of a government by and for its people. *All* its people."[22]

The third phase of the Depression began in 1937, when the Roosevelt administration, wanting to burnish its conservative credentials, ill-advisedly sought to balance the budget, and to do so by raising taxes and cutting government spending. The result was a recession within a depression. Yet coincidental with the new economic downturn, the dark clouds of world war loomed overhead. Government spending eventually soared to meet the need for armaments and, soon enough, fighting men. The war ended the Great Depression by taking government spending and stimulation to a whole new level. And, above all, it brought people and the country together in a common effort to fight a common foe.

As Morris Dickstein points out in his wonderful book, *Dancing in the Dark*, one of the last major films of the thirties, *The Wizard of Oz* (1939), clearly illustrates the collective energy that had become evident during the Great Depression and with the coming of war. Once Dorothy is transported from the rural poverty of her Kansas homeland to the other world of ravishing beauty but constant fear, she realizes that the only way home is through working with others in a cooperative effort. The characters in the film must display the qualities demanded to get through the Depression, "those FDR was trying to instill: courage to face up to the social crisis, empathy for the suffering of others, a break with past thinking about how we ought to live."[23] By doing so, Americans may not have reached a trouble-free world, "somewhere over the rainbow," but they could at least look forward to brighter tomorrows.

CHRONOLOGY

1929   **October 29** On "Black Tuesday" the stock market crashes, losing an estimated $30 million in stock values by mid-November and ushering in the Great Depression.

1930   **March** More than 2.2 million people are unemployed.

November Nearly 6,000 unemployed individuals in New York City are selling apples on street corners for five cents apiece.

1931   **February** Food riots break out in parts of the United States, with individuals breaking into grocery markets to steal fruit, canned goods, bacon, and ham.

May 1 The Empire State Building, the premier Art Deco office building, opens for business.

December New York's Bank of the United States, with deposits of more than $200 million, collapses.

1932   **January** Congress establishes the Reconstruction Finance Corporation (RFC) to lend $2 billion to banks, insurance companies, and building and loan associations.

May 3 Farmers in the Midwest, led by activist Milo Reno, form the Farmer's Holiday Association (FHA).

July Violence erupts when Hoover orders federal troops, under the command of General Douglas MacArthur, to break up Bonus Army demonstrators.

November Franklin Delano Roosevelt (FDR), a Democrat, is elected president in a landslide over Herbert Hoover, a Republican.

1933   **March** FDR announces a four-day bank holiday to begin Monday, March 6.

1933   April The Civilian Conservation Corps (CCC) is established, designed to give relief to unemployed men between the ages of 17 and 27.

May The National Industrial Recover Act (NIRA) is introduced into Congress. The Tennessee Valley Authority (TVA) is created as a federally run hydroelectric power program. The Agricultural Adjustment Act (AAA) is authorized by Congress.

June An estimated 25 percent of the labor force is unemployed.

December Prohibition is repealed with passage of the Twenty-first Amendment to the Constitution.

TIMELINE

1929

October 29 On "Black Tuesday" the stock market crashes, losing an estimated $30 million in stock values by mid-November and ushering in the Great Depression.

1932

November Franklin Delano Roosevelt (FDR), a Democrat, is elected president in a landslide over Herbert Hoover, a Republican.

1929 ──────── **1933**

1933

April The Civilian Conservation Corps (CCC) is established, designed to give relief to unemployed men between the ages of 17 and 27.

May The National Industrial Recover Act (NIRA) is introduced into Congress. The Tennessee Valley Authority (TVA) is created as a federally run hydroelectric power program. The Agricultural Adjustment Act (AAA) is authorized by Congress.

1934   **May** A three-day dust storm blows an estimated 350 million tons of soil off the land in the Midwest.

May 9 Longshoremen in every West Coast port go out on strike.

May 23 The infamous bank-robbing Bonnie and Clyde are gunned down in a police ambush.

August 22 The conservative American Liberty League is formed, led by wealthy anti-New Deal businessmen.

1935   **April** FDR signs legislation creating the Works Progress Administration (WPA) that would eventually put more than 8.5 million individuals to work.

July FDR signs the Wagner National Labor Relations Act.

1935

April FDR signs legislation creating the Works Progress Administration (WPA) that would eventually put more than 8.5 million individuals to work.

August The Social Security Act of 1935 is signed into law by FDR.

1940

November 7 FDR defeats Wendell Willkie to win an unprecedented third term as president.

1935

1941

1936

January The U.S. Supreme Court rules the AAA unconstitutional.

November FDR is elected to a second term, winning every state except Maine and Vermont.

1941

December 7 Japanese attack Pearl Harbor, drawing the United States into war, and effectively ending the Great Depression.

1935   **July 14** First ever general strike called in San Francisco, California.

August The Social Security Act of 1935 is signed into law by FDR.

September 8 Huey Long of Louisiana is shot and dies 30 hours later.

December Townsend clubs claim a combined membership of more than 2.2 million.

1936   **January** The U.S. Supreme Court rules the AAA unconstitutional.

March Photographer Dorothea Lange, visiting a pea pickers' camp in California, photographs "Migrant Mother."

October Author John Steinbeck begins a series of articles on the plight of California migrant workers for the *San Francisco News*.

November FDR is elected to a second term, winning every state except Maine and Vermont.

1937   **January** United Automobile Workers strike at the General Motors plant in Flint, Michigan.

March A recession within the Depression begins as unemployment rises.

April 12 The Supreme Court declares provisions of the NLRA unconstitutional.

July 2 Amelia Earhart and her navigator are lost over the Pacific.

1938   **June** Economy begins to recover again.

1939   **March** John Steinbeck's novel about migrant workers, *The Grapes of Wrath*, is published to wide acclaim.

September World War II begins in Europe.

1940   November 7 FDR defeats Wendell Willkie to win an unprecedented third term as president.

December FDR declares in a fireside chat, "We must be the arsenal of democracy."

1941   December 7 Japanese attack Pearl Harbor, drawing the United States into war, and effectively ending the Great Depression.

NOTES

CHAPTER ONE

1. Frederick Lewis Allen, *Since Yesterday: The 1930s in America September 3, 1929–September 3, 1939*. New York: Harper & Row, 1939, pp. 61–62.
2. Nick Taylor, *American-Made: The Enduring Legacy of the WPA When FDR Put the Nation to Work*. New York: Bantam Books, 2009, p. 10.
3. Caroline Bird, *The Invisible Scar: The Great Depression, and What It Did to American Life, from Then Until Now*. New York: David McKay Company, 1966, p. 35.
4. Ibid., p. 34.
5. Nick Taylor, *American-Made*, p. 9.
6. Eric Rauchway, *The Great Depression & the New Deal*. Oxford: Oxford University Press, 2008, p. 40.
7. Caroline Bird, *The Invisible Scar*, pp. 48–49.
8. Columbia Encyclopedia, *Great Depression*. New York: Columbia University Press, 2001–2008, p. 1.
9. Caroline Bird, *The Invisible Scar*, p. 30.
10. Eric Rauchway, *The Great Depression & the New Deal*, p. 39.
11. Studs Terkel, *Hard Times*. New York: The New Press, 1970, p. 5.
12. "Jobless Couple Starving; Constable Finds Them in Summer Cottage Near Up-State Lake," *New York Times*, December 25, 1931, p. 27.
13. Caroline Bird, *The Invisible Scar*, p. 35.
14. Studs Terkel, *Hard Times*, p. 41.
15. Ibid., p. 93.
16. Eric Rauchway, *The Great Depression & the New Deal*, p. 50.
17. John D. Weaver, *Bonus March*. American Heritage Publishing, 2008, p. 4. AmericanHeritage.com.
18. Nick Taylor, *American-Made*, p. 55.

CHAPTER TWO

1. Frederick Lewis Allen, *Only Yesterday: An Informal History of the 1920's*. New York: Harper & Row, 1931, p. 27.
2. Ibid., p. 36.
3. Ibid., p. 70.
4. Ibid., p. 77.
5. Ibid., p. 246.
6. Ibid., p. 142.
7. Eric Rauchway, *The Great Depression & the New Deal*, p. 13.
8. Sharon Murphy, *The Advertising of Installment Plans*. Charlottesville: Corcoran Department of History at the University of Virginia, 1995, p.1.
9. Ibid., p. 2.
10. Eric Rauchway, *The Great Depression & the New Deal*, p. 9.
11. Paul H. Jeffers, *The Complete Idiot's Guide to the Great Depression*. New York: Penguin Group, 2002, p. 12.
12. Adam Cohen, *Nothing to Fear: FDR's Inner Circle and the Hundred Days That Created*

Modern America. New York: Penguin Group, 2009, p. 48.

13. David Colbert, *Eyewitness to Wall Street*. New York: Broadway Books, 2001, p. 125.
14. Ibid., p. 126.
15. Paul H. Jeffers, *The Complete Idiot's Guide to the Great Depression*, p. 22.
16. Eric Rauchway, *The Great Depression & the New Deal*, p. 18.
17. Ibid.
18. David Colbert, *Eyewitness to Wall Street*, p. 133.
19. Ibid., p.136.

CHAPTER THREE

1. Roger Biles, *A New Deal for the American People*. Dekalb: Northern Illinois University Press, 1991, p. 8.
2. Eric Rauchway, *The Great Depression & the New Deal*, p. 19.
3. Ibid.
4. Frederick Lewis Allen, *Only Yesterday*, pp. 208–209.
5. Paul Jeffers, *The Complete Idiot's Guide to the Great Depression*, p. 52.
6. Nick Taylor, *American-Made*, p. 25.
7. Ibid., p. 27.
8. Caroline Bird, *The Invisible Scar*, p. 84.
9. Paul H. Jeffers, *The Complete Idiot's Guide to the Great Depression*, p. 53.
10. Ronald A. Reis, *The World Trade Organization*. New York: Chelsea House Publishers, 2009, p. 23.
11. Amity Shlaes, *The Forgotten Man*. New York: Harper Perennial, 2008, p. 95.

12. Ibid.
13. Nick Taylor, *American-Made*, pp. 28–29.
14. Eric Rauchway, *The Great Depression & the New Deal*, p. 39.
15. Nick Taylor, *American-Made*, p. 12.
16. Eric Rauchway, *The Great Depression & the New Deal*, p. 35.
17. Nick Taylor, *American-Made*, p. 89.
18. Ibid.

CHAPTER FOUR

1. James MacGregor Burns, *Roosevelt: The Lion and the Fox*. New York: Harcourt, Brace and Company, 1956, p. 87.
2. Ronald A. Reis, *Jonas Salk*. New York: Ferguson, 2006, p. 3.
3. James MacGregor Burns, *Roosevelt*, p. 88.
4. Ibid.
5. Nick Taylor, *American-Made*, p. 79.
6. Franklin D. Roosevelt, *Fireside Chat on Banking*, March 12, 1933, p. 1. Available online at http://www.presidency.ucsb.edu/ws/index.php?pid=14540.
7. Ibid., p. 3.
8. Paul H. Jeffers, *The Complete Idiot's Guide to the Great Depression*, p. 41.
9. Ibid., p. 42
10. Adam Cohen, *Nothing to Fear*, p. 127.
11. Ibid., p. 299.
12. Ronald A. Reis, *The Dust Bowl*. New York: Chelsea House Publishers, 2008, p. 60.
13. Eric Dodds and Rebecca Kaplan, "An Enduring New Deal," *Time*, July 6, 2009, p. 36.

14. Alonzo L. Hamby, *For the Survival of Democracy.* New York: Simon and Schuster, 1994, p. 164.
15. Eric Rauchway, *The Great Depression & the New Deal*, p. 85.

CHAPTER FIVE

1. David Von Drehle, *Triangle: The Fire That Changed America.* New York: Grove Press, 2003, pp. 194–195.
2. Kirstin Downey, *The Women Behind the New Deal: The Life of Frances Perkins, FDR's Secretary of Labor and His Moral Conscience.* New York: Doubleday, 2009, p. 34.
3. Ibid.
4. Kristin Downey, *The Women Behind the New Deal*, p. 36.
5. David Von Drehle, *Triangle*, p. 195.
6. Ibid., p. 215.
7. Ibid.
8. Kristin Downey, *The Women Behind the New Deal*, p. 109.
9. Ibid., p. 115.
10. Ibid., p. 120.
11. Ibid., p. 123.
12. Ibid., p. 124.
13. T.H. Watkins, *The Great Depression: America in the 1930s.* Boston: Little, Brown, 1993, p. 13.
14. Kristin Downey, *The Women Behind the New Deal*, p. 239.
15. Ibid., p. 216.

CHAPTER SIX

1. Morris Dickstein, *Dancing in the Dark: A Cultural History of the Great Depression.* New York: W.W. Norton & Company, 2009, p. 219.
2. Caroline Bird, *The Invisible Scar*, p. 101.

3. Peter Filene, *American Families During the Great Depression.* p. 2. Available online at http://www.klt.ncssm.edu/lmtm/docs/families/script.pdf.
4. Ibid.
5. Ibid., p. 3.
6. Nick Taylor, *American-Made*, p. 107.
7. Edwin G. Hill, *In the Shadow of the Mountain: The Spirit of the CCC.* Pullman: Washington State University Press, 1990, p. 33.
8. Frank C. Davis, *My C.C.C. Days: Memories of the Civilian Conservation Corps.* Boone, N.C.: Parkway Publishers, 2006, p. 7.
9. Ibid., p. 8.
10. Ibid., p. 26.
11. Edwin G. Hill, *In the Shadow of the Mountain*, pp. 138–139.
12. Nick Taylor, *American-Made*, p. 3.
13. Ibid., pp. 189–190.
14. Eric Rauchway, *The Great Depression & the New Deal*, p. 68.
15. Nick Taylor, *American-Made*, p. 215.
16. Ibid., p. 168.
17. Ibid.
18. Paul H. Jeffers, *The Complete Idiot's Guide to the Great Depression*, p. 89.
19. Ibid., p. 90.
20. Nick Taylor, *American-Made*, p. 182.
21. Ibid., pp. 182–183.

CHAPTER SEVEN

1. Adam Cohen, *Nothing to Fear*, p. 125.
2. Ronald A. Reis, *The Dust Bowl*, p. 52.

3. David McCullough, *Surviving the Dust Bowl*. Enhanced Transcript. Available online at http://www.pbs.org/wgbh/amex/dustbowl/filmmore/transcripat/index.html.
4. Ronald A. Reis, *The Dust Bowl*, p. 78.
5. John Steinbeck, *The Grapes of Wrath*. New York: Penguin Books, 1939, p. 233.
6. Ronald A. Reis, *The Dust Bowl*, p. 84.
7. Ibid., p. 86.
8. John Steinbeck, "The Harvest Gypsies," *San Francisco News*, October 7, 1936.
9. John Steinbeck, *The Grapes of Wrath*, p. 246.
10. John Steinbeck, "The Harvest Gypsies."
11. Ibid.
12. Ibid.
13. Ibid.
14. Karen Tsujimoto, *Dorothea Lange: Archive of an Artist*. Oakland: Oakland Museum of California, 1995, p. 11.
15. Ibid.
16. Mark Durden, *Dorothea Lange*. New York: Phaidon Press, 2001, p. 12.

CHAPTER EIGHT

1. Nick Taylor, *American-Made*, p. 153.
2. Eric Rauchway, *The Great Depression & the New Deal*, p. 126.
3. Ibid., p. 108.
4. Caroline Bird, *The Invisible Scar*, p. 219.
5. Paul H. Jeffers, *The Great Depression*, p. 189.
6. Ibid.

7. Adam Cohen, *Nothing to Fear*, p. 284.
8. Glenda Elizabeth Gilmore, *Defying Dixie: The Radical Roots of Civil Rights, 1919–1950*. New York: W.W. Norton & Company, 2008, p. 120.
9. Robert Bendiner, *Just Around the Corner: A Highly Selective History of the Thirties*. New York: Harper & Row, Publishers, 1967, p. 134.
10. Frederick Lewis Allen, *Since Yesterday*, p. 190.
11. Amity Shlaes, *The Forgotten Man: A New History of the Great Depression*. New York: Harper Perennial, 2007, p. 248.
12. "Charles Coughlin." Available online at http://www.answers.com/topic/charles-coughlin.
13. Ibid., p. 3.
14. Ibid., p. 4.
15. Paul H. Jeffers, *The Great Depression*, p. 177.
16. Ibid.
17. Robert Bendiner, *Just Around the Corner*, p. 127.
18. Ibid., p. 130.

CHAPTER NINE

1. Morris Dickstein, *Dancing in the Dark*. p. xix
2. Ibid., p. 438.
3. Bing Crosby. *The Official Home of Bing Crosby*. Available online at http://www.bingcrosby.com.
4. Morris Dickstein, *Dancing in the Dark*, p. 414.
5. Ibid., p. 416.
6. Ibid.
7. Ibid.
8. Caroline Bird, *The Invisible Scar*, pp. 61–62.
9. Ibid., pp. 64–65.

10. Laura Hillenbrand, *Seabiscuit: An American Legend.* New York: Ballantine Books, 2001, p. vii.
11. Paul H. Jeffers, *The Great Depression,* p. 216.
12. Ibid., p. 220.
13. Donald M. Goldstein and Katherine V. Dillon, *Amelia: The Centennial Biography of an Aviation Pioneer.* Washington, D.C.: Brassey's, 1997, pp. 8–9.
14. Amelia Earhart, *Last Flight.* New York: Harcourt, Brace and Company (first edition: Putnam), 1937, p. 4.
15. Seth Goddard, "Life Hero of the Week Profile—Amelia Earhart—First Lady of the Sky." Available online at www.life.com.

CHAPTER TEN

1. *The Great Depression Statistics by the Numbers.* Available online at http://www.shmoop.com/great-depression/statistics.html.
2. Ibid.
3. Ibid.
4. Nick Taylor, *American-Made,* p. 452.
5. Kirstin Downey, *The Woman Behind the New Deal,* p. 292.
6. Nick Taylor, *American-Made,* p. 450.
7. Ibid., p. 451.
8. Peter Beinart, "The Price of World Peace." *Time,* July 6, 2009, p. 49.
9. Ibid.
10. Nick Taylor, *American-Made,* p. 466.
11. Erick Rauchway, *The Great Depression & the New Deal,* p. 126.
12. Nick Taylor, *American-Made,* p. 490.
13. Paul H. Jeffers, *The Great Depression,* p. 306.
14. Peter Beinart, "The Price of World Peace," p. 49.
15. Paul H. Jeffers, *The Great Depression,* p. 306.
16. Nick Taylor, *American-Made,* p. 509.
17. Ibid., p. 510.
18. Ibid., p. 513.
19. Kirstin Downey, *The Woman Behind the New Deal,* p. 320.
20. Ibid.
21. Ibid., p. 323.
22. Nick Taylor, *American-Made,* p. 530.
23. Morris Dickstein, *Dancing in the Dark,* p. 524.

BIBLIOGRAPHY

Allen, Frederick Lewis. *Only Yesterday*. New York: Harper & Row, 1931.

———. *Since Yesterday*. New York: Harper & Row, 1939.

Allen, Frederick Lewis, and Agnes Rogers. *I Remember Distinctly: A Family Album of the American People in the Years of Peace, 1918 to Pearl Harbor*. New York: Harper, 1947.

Alter, Jonathan A. *The Defining Moment: FDR's Hundred Days and the Triumph of Hope*. New York: Simon & Schuster, 2006.

Bellush, Bernard. *The Failure of the NRA*. New York: W.W. Norton, 1975.

Bendiner, Robert. *Just Around the Corner: A Highly Selective History of the Thirties*. New York: Harper & Row, 1967.

Bergman, Andrew. *We're in the Money: Depression America and Its Films*. New York: New York University Press, 1971.

Biles, Roger. *A New Deal for the American People*. DeKalb: Northern Illinois University Press, 1991.

Bird, Caroline. *The Invisible Scar: The Great Depression, and What It Did to American Life, from Then Until Now*. New York: David McKay Company, 1966.

Burns, James MacGregor. *Roosevelt: The Lion and the Fox*. New York: Harcourt, Brace and Company, 1956.

Christman, Henry M., ed. *Kingfish to America: Share Our Wealth; Selected Senatorial Papers of Huey P. Long*. New York: Schocken, 1985.

Cohen, Adam. *Nothing to Fear: FDR's Inner Circle and the Hundred Days That Created Modern America*. New York: The Penguin Press, 2009.

Colbert, David. *Eyewitness to Wall Street: Four Hundred Years of Dreamers, Schemers, Busts and Booms*. New York: Broadway Books, 2001.

Columbia Encyclopedia. *Great Depression*. New York: Columbia University Press, 2008.

Cooper, Michael L. *Dust to Eat: Drought and Depression in the 1930s*. New York: Clarion Books, 2004.

Davis, Frank C. *My C.C.C. Days: Memories of the Civilian Conservation Corps*. Boone, N.C.: Parkway Publishers, 2006.

Downey, Kirstin. *The Woman Behind the New Deal: The Life of Frances Perkins, FDR's Secretary of Labor and His Moral Conscience*. New York: Doubleday, 2009.

Durden, Mark. *Dorothea Lange*. New York: Phaidon Press Limited, 2001.

Earhart, Amelia. *Last Flight*. New York: Harcourt, Brace and Company, 1937.

Egan, Timothy. *The Worst Hard Times: The Untold Story of Those Who Survived the Great American Dust Bowl*. Boston: Houghton Mifflin Company, 2006.

Ferguson, Niall. *The Ascent of Money: A Financial History of the World*. New York: Penguin Books, 2008.

Flanagan, Hallie. *Arena: The Story of the Federal Theater*. New York: Limelight, 1985.

Flynn, Sean Masaki. *Economics for Dummies*. Hoboken, N.J.: Wiley Publishing, 2005.

Gabree, John. *Gangsters: From Little Caesar to the Godfather*. New York: Gallahad Books, 1973.

Galbraith, John Kenneth. *The Great Crash 1929*. Boston: Houghton Mifflin Company, 1954.

Gilmore, Glenda Elizabeth. *Defying Dixie: The Radical Roots of Civil Rights, 1919–1950*. New York: W.W. Norton & Company, 2008.

Goldstein, Donald M., and Katherine V. Dillon. *Amelia: The Centennial Biography of an Aviation Pioneer*. Washington, D.C.: Brassey's. 1997.

Gordon, Thomas, and Max Morgan-Witts. *The Day the Bubble Burst: A Social History of the Wall Street Crash of 1929*. Garden City: Doubleday & Company, 1979.

Hamby, Alonzo L. *For the Survival of Democracy*. New York: Simon and Schuster, 1994.

Henderson, Caroline. *Letters from the Dust Bowl*. Norman: University of Oklahoma Press, 2001.

Hill, Edwin G. *In the Shadow of the Mountain: The Spirit of the CCC*. Pullman: Washington State University Press, 1990.

Hillenbrand, Laura. *Seabiscuit: An American Legend*. New York: Ballantine Books, 2001.

Janke, Katelan. *Survival in the Storm: The Dust Bowl Diary of Grace Edwards*. New York: Scholastic, 2002.

Jeffers, Paul H. *The Complete Idiot's Guide to the Great Depression*. New York: The Penguin Group, 2002.

La Chapelle, Peter. *Proud to Be an Okie: Cultural Politics, Country Music, and Migration to Southern California*. Berkeley: University of California Press, 2007.

Lash, Joseph P. *Dealers and Dreamers: A New Look at the New Deal*. New York: Doubleday, 1988.

Long, Huey. *Every Man a King: The Autobiography of Huey Long*. New Orleans: National Book Co., 1933.

Lovell, Mary S. *The Sound of Wings: The Life of Amelia Earhart.* New York: St. Martin's Griffin, 2009.

Okrent, Daniel. *Great Fortune: The Epic of Rockefeller Center.* New York: The Penguin Group, 2003.

Partridge, Elisabeth. *This Land Was Made for You and Me: The Life and Songs of Woody Guthrie.* New York: Viking, 2002.

Rauchway, Eric. *The Great Depression & the New Deal: A Very Short Introduction.* Oxford: Oxford University Press, 2008.

Reis, Ronald A. *The World Trade Organization.* New York: Chelsea House Publishers, 2009.

———. *The Dust Bowl.* New York: Chelsea House Publishers, 2008.

Roosevelt, Eleanor. *My Day: The Best of Eleanor Roosevelt's Acclaimed Newspaper Columns, 1936–1962.* Edited by David Emblidge. New York: Da Capo Press, 2001.

Schlesinger, Arthur A. Jr. *The Coming of the New Deal.* Boston: Houghton Mifflin Co., 1958.

Shlaes, Amity. *The Forgotten Man: A New History of the Great Depression.* New York: Harper Perennial. 2007.

Stanley, Jerry. *Children of the Dust Bowl: The True Story of the School at Weedpatch Camp.* New York: Crown Publishers, 1992.

Steinbeck, John. *The Grapes of Wrath.* New York: Penguin Books, 1939.

Taylor, Nick. *American-Made: The Enduring Legacy of the WPA: When FDR Put the Nation to Work.* New York: Bantam Books, 2009.

Terkel, Studs. *Hard Times: An Oral History of the Great Depression.* New York: The New Press, 1986.

Tsujimoto, Karen. *Dorothea Lange: Archive of an Artist.* Oakland: Oakland Museum of California, 1995.

Von Drehle, David. *Triangle: The Fire That Changed America.* New York: Grove Press, 2003.

Watkins, T.H. *The Great Depression: America in the 1930s.* New York: Little, Brown and Company, 1993.

Wilson, Edmund. *The American Earthquake: A Documentary of the Jazz Age, the Great Depression, and the New Deal.* Garden City, N.Y.: Doubleday & Company, 1958.

Wunder, John R., Frances W. Kaye, and Vernon Carstensen, eds. *Americans View Their Dust Bowl Experience.* Boulder: University Press of Colorado, 2001.

NEWSPAPERS AND MAGAZINES

"Colorado Families Flee Dust Storms." *New York Times,* March 25, 1935.

Dodds, Eric, and Rebecca Kaplan. "An Enduring New Deal." *Time,* July 6, 2009.

"Jobless Couple Starving; Constable Finds Them in Summer Cottage Near Up-State Lake." *New York Times,* December 25, 1931.

Ramo, Joshua Cooper. "Unemployment Nation." *Time,* September 21, 2009.

Steinbeck, John. "The Harvest Gypsies." *San Francisco News,* October 7, 1936.

FILM

American Experience: Surviving the Dust Bowl. WGBH Boston, 2007.

Just the Facts: Emergence of Modern America-The Great Depression. Cerebellum Corp., 2001.

Our Daily Bread and Other Great Films of the Great Depression. Image Entertainment, 1999.

The Great Depression. A&E, 2009.

The Panic Is On: The Great Depression as Seen by the Common Man. Shanachie, 2009.

The Plow That Broke the Plains, The MARPAT Foundation. 2005.

WEB SITES

American Families During the Great Depression
http://www.klt.ncssm.edu/lmtm/docs/families/script.pdf

American Heritage Publishing, Bonus March
http://staging.americanheritage.com/articles/magazine/ah/1963/4/1963_4_18.shtml

America's Great Depression
http://www.amatecon.com/greatdepression.html

Charles Coughlin Biography
http://www.answers.com/topic/charles-coughlin

Farming in the 1930s
http://www.livinghistoryfarm.org

Franklin D. Roosevelt, Fireside Chat on Banking, March 12, 1933
http://www.presidency.ucsb.edu/ws/index.php?pid=14540

Franklin D. Roosevelt Presidential Library and Museum
http://docs.fkrilibrary.marist.edu/firesi90.html

The Great Depression Statistics by the Numbers
http://www.shmoop.com/great-depression/statistics.html

Main Causes of the Great Depression
http://www.gusmorino.com/pag3/greatderpression/index.html

The Museum of Broadcast Communications
http://www.museum.tv/exhibitionssection.php?page=79

The Official Home of Bing Crosby

http://www.bingcrosby.com

Slouching Towards Utopia?: The Economic History of the Twentieth Century: The Great Crash and the Great Slump

http://econ161.berkeley.edu/TCEH/Slouch_Crash14.html

Surviving the Dust Bowl

http://www.pbs.org/wgbh/amex/dustbowl/filmmore/transcripat/index.html

FURTHER READING

Cooper, Michael L. *Dust to Eat: Drought and Depression in the 1930s.* New York: Clarion Books, 2004.

Hopkinson, Deborah, and James E. Ransome. *Sky Boys: How They Built the Empire State Building.* New York: Schwartz & Wade Books, 2006.

Isaacs, Sally Senzell. *America in the Time of Franklin Delano Roosevelt: 1929 to 1948.* New York: Heinemann Library, 1999.

Janke, Katelan. *Survival in the Storm: The Dust Bowl Diary of Grace Edwards.* New York: Scholastic, 2002.

Rich, Doris L. *Amelia Earhart.* Washington D.C.: Smithsonian Press, 1996.

Stanley, Jerry. *Children of the Dust Bowl: The True Story of the School at Weedpatch Camp.* New York: Crown Publishers, 1992.

WEB SITES

About the Great Depression

http://www.english.illinois.edu/maps/depression/about.htm

A good summary of the causes and consequences of the Great Depression, with emphasis on its worldwide impact.

America from the Great Depression to World War II: Photographs from the FSA-OWI, 1935–1945

http://rs6.loc.gov/fsowhome.html

A collection of images in the Farm Security Administration Office presents some of the most famous documentary photographs ever produced.

The Great Depression.

http://www.42explore2.com/depresn.htm

Presents both a quick overview of the subject and a more in-depth analysis.

The Great Depression (1929–1939). Eleanor Roosevelt National Historic Site

http://www.nps.gov/archive/elro/glossary/great-depression.htm

A good presentation of the overall effects of the Great Depression on American life.

Great Depression Pictures.

http://history1900s.about.com/od/photographs/tp/great depressionpictures.htm

A collection of pictures of the Great Depression, offering glimpse into the lives of those who suffered the most.

PHOTO CREDITS

INDEX

ABOUT THE AUTHOR

RONALD A. REIS has written young adult biographies of Eugenie Clark, Jonas Salk, Mickey Mantle, Ted Williams, Sitting Bull, Buffalo Bill Cody, Simón Bolívar, and Valentino, as well as books about the Dust Bowl, the New York City subway system, the Empire State Building, African Americans and the Civil War, and the World Trade Organization. He is a Western Writers of America Spur Award Winner.